The Yale Building Project: The First 40 Years

The Yale Building Project: The First 40 Years

Richard W. Hayes

Foreword by Robert A.M. Stern

Yale School of Architecture

Distributed by Yale University Press, New Haven and London

Yale School of Architecture
180 York Street
New Haven, Connecticut 06520

Published by the Yale School of Architecture
Distributed by Yale University Press, New Haven and London
Yale University Press
P.O. Box 209040
New Haven, CT 06520-9040
www.yalebooks.com

Editor: Nina Rappaport, Director of Publications,
Yale School of Architecture

Design: mgmt. design, Brooklyn, New York

We would like to thank William Grover ('69), Jefferson Riley ('72), Mark
Simon ('72), J. P. Chadwick Floyd ('73), and James Childress, Partners at
Centerbrook Architects and Planners, as well as Marc Appleton ('72),
for their ongoing support of the Charles W. Moore Building Program
Fund, established in 1995 by Charles Moore's partners, colleagues,
students, clients and friends, which assists the First-Year Building Project
Summer Interns. We also thank Tai Soo Kim ('62) for endowing the Tai
Soo Kim Partners Summer Internship Fund, and James Stewart Polshek
('55) and Polshek Partnership Architects for their annual support for a
summer intern.

We would like to acknowledge the support of Philip B. Svigals ('76) for
his support of this book. We would also like to acknowledge the Ruther-
ford Trowbridge Memorial Publication Fund; the Paul Rudolph Publication
Fund, established by Claire and Maurits Edersheim; the Robert A.M.
Stern Fund, established by Judy and Walter Hunt ('76); the Nitkin Family
Dean's Discretionary Fund in Architecture; and the James Wilder Green
Dean's Resource Fund.

Library of Congress Control Number: 2007923907
ISBN: 978-0-300-12316-6
A catalog record for this book is available from the Library of Congress.

Contents

Foreword
Robert A.M. Stern

The First-Year Building Project at the Yale School of Architecture is a unique achievement in the history of American architectural education, for forty years contributing to the education of many of the country's leading architects. It has served as a model for similar efforts at other schools, and inspired many architects to devote their career to those at the social margins. The Building Project began in the late 1960s during an important and critical era in American culture. Its origins reflect a period of intense social activism when students wanted "to make a difference" by taking direct action to improve the world. While it has remained true to its original spirit of direct action, the Building Project has evolved, mirroring changes in American culture. Projects have ranged from community centers built during the 1960s in rural and impoverished Appalachia to pavilions and recreational structures built in the 1980s throughout Connecticut. Recently, students in the Building Project have constructed affordable housing in New Haven in conjunction with Habitat for Humanity and Neighborhood Housing Services, thereby helping to stabilize neighborhoods.

From its initial formulation during the 1966–67 academic year until the present, the pedagogical structure of the Building Project has changed remarkably little: during the spring semester of their first year of graduate study, Yale architecture students work directly with a community-based client to realize an actual building. Following a design competition in which all class members participate, the students collaborate on a selected design, which they proceed to build during the spring and summer months after classes end. The Building Project, with its mixture of design, construction technology, and social interaction, fosters an understanding of architecture as a dialogue among diverse groups working toward a common goal. In the course of the Building Project, students learn how to work with clients, develop programs into realizable designs, translate their designs into technical drawings, manage construction, and actually build their own work.

While the group dynamic and the sense of social responsibility embedded in the Building Project are crucial to its success, it is an act of seeing a design through to construction that has the most profound effect on the training of fledgling architects. The fundamental reality of the Building Project makes it unique. In learning by doing, the study of architecture moves from abstraction to reality in ways that anticipate professional practice. When the program began, the hands-on approach reflected a significant trend in the profession. Today, the trend is toward increasing prefabrication, so the pedagogy has evolved to enable students not only to pound nails in the field but also to explore new digital fabrication technologies. This increases students' understanding of construction, in terms of how materials are used, how structures are built, as well as the design of specific details. The computer does not overwhelm the process but is absorbed into it.

This book consists of two historical essays by Richard W. Hayes and an interview with Paul B. Brouard who has been closely involved with the Building Project as a faculty member since 1971, followed by descriptions of each of the projects written by a team of graduates and current students. Each year I am impressed by the quality of the students' designs, yet each year they seem to get even better. This book is a wonderful opportunity to salute the work of our students and faculty as the Yale Building Project continues forward.

Acknowledgments
Richard W. Hayes and Nina Rappaport

"You are always in debt," wrote the American poet Delmore Schwartz, and we have learned the truth of Schwartz's insight in the course of preparing this book. We would like to take this opportunity to thank the institutions and people who helped us.

The book was undertaken at the suggestion of Robert A.M. Stern, Dean and J.M. Hoppin Professor at the Yale School of Architecture; it is due to his vision and commitment that this publication has been realized. Dean Stern also initiated an effort to archive the material collected in the course of our research. We would like to thank Michelle Komie of Yale University Press and her colleagues for distributing the book. Associate Dean John D. Jacobson made sure that everything ran smoothly. Jean F. Sielaff, Senior Administrative Assistant to the Dean, and Richard DeFlumeri, Special Events Coordinator, unfailingly responded in a thorough manner to all of our inquiries.

Richard W. Hayes's research began as an independent study in 2002 at Brown University with Dietrich Neumann whom he would like to thank for his encouragement and interest. Hayes's work was supported by grants from the American Institute of Architects and the American Architectural Foundation, and he would like to thank the Foundation's Donald I. King and Mary Felber for their help. An all-too-brief residence at the MacDowell Colony in 2005 gave Hayes a respite from practicing as an architect in New York in order to work on this project.

We would like to thank contributing author Ted Whitten, whose indefatigable research deserves special recognition, and photo editor Marc Guberman for his remarkable organizational and management skills; as well as Tim Applebee, Marissa Brown, April Clark, Tarra Cotterman, Jeff Goldstein, Abigail Ransmeier, Adam Ruedig, Vanessa Ruff, and Benjamin Smoot for their work. Paul B. Brouard carefully read each of the project descriptions and made numerous contributions; he well deserves the affection and gratitude of generations of Yale students. Sarah Gephart of mgmt. design designed a beautiful book, while Ann Holcomb went above and beyond the call of duty as copy editor.

Herbert S. Newman kindly found the time to discuss his central role in the first forty years of the Yale Building Project. On two separate occasions, Kent and Nona Bloomer and Felix and Jeanne Drury prepared delicious meals for Hayes during lengthy interviews; their hospitality was as welcome as their tack-sharp memories. Turner Brooks, F. Andrus Burr, Steve Edwins, James Volney Righter, Herman D.J. Spiegel, and Robert Swenson read early drafts of Hayes's essay and offered pertinent criticisms. Our research could not have been completed without the help of Marc Appleton, Mack Caldwell, Tom Carey, Michael G. Curtis, Mark J. Ellis, Sonya Hals, James Kessler, Ellen R. Leopold, Kevin Lichten, Marvin Michalsen, Nancy Monroe, Reese Owens, Donald E. Raney, Gitta Robinson, Daniel V. Scully, David E. Sellers, Mark Simon, Barry Svigals, and Brink Thorne, who responded to many queries and loaned personal documents. Denise Scott Brown and Hugh Hardy discussed the nineteen-sixties with Hayes. Kevin Keim made the resources of the Charles W. Moore Center for the Study of Place available to us. Clyde Carpenter and Ray Gindroz confirmed facts. We would also like to thank Judy Throm of the Archives of American Art at the Smithsonian Institution, Jennie Benford of the Carnegie Mellon University Archives, and the staffs of Manuscripts and Archives, Yale University Library, and the Avery Architectural and Fine Arts Library at Columbia University.

Finally, we would like to extend a heartfelt thank you to all of the alumni of the Yale School of Architecture who answered our questions and shared their memories throughout our work on this book. We list them at the end.

9

Learning, Building: Charles W. Moore
and the First-Year Building Project

*For the opportunity...to create a public realm, we must look to sources other
than the Establishment, to people or institutions interested at once in public
activity and in place.*
—Charles W. Moore,1965[1]

In 1965, the president of Yale University, Kingman Brewster, Jr., invited
architect Charles W. Moore to become the chairman of the University's
Department of Architecture.[2] Moore, forty years old, was then chairman of
the Department of Architecture at the Berkeley campus of the University
of California, and had developed a reputation as an innovative educator.
Moore went on to provide a decade's worth of leadership at Yale—first
as chairman, then as dean once the department became an independent
graduate school, and later as faculty member—during a tumultuous and
critical time in the history of Yale and of American culture. One of Moore's
most significant accomplishments at Yale was the creation, in 1967, of what
was initially called the "First-Year Building Project." As part of this program,
members of the first-year class designed, as a group effort, a building that
they later constructed in the course of the spring semester and the summer following the end of classes. Forty years later, this program continues
to be a vital component of the Yale curriculum and a unique achievement
in the education of architects in America. The Yale Building Project, as
the program is now called, is important from several perspectives: for its
pedagogic role in the professional training of architects; as an expression
of Moore's own educational views; as a manifestation of the role of prag-
matism in American culture; and as a reflection of a period of heightened
social activism and dramatic institutional change.

Background
Born in 1925, Charles W. Moore was a leading architect and theorist of the
postmodern movement of the 1970s and 1980s. While some view Moore
as an enigmatic and elusive figure, most of his peers agree that he was one
of the most vital educators of his time.[3] Architecture critic Martin Filler,
for example, described Moore as "the most influential architecture professor of his generation. Unlike many other star architects, he was also a
great teacher, and for over forty years he imparted his vast knowledge and
passionate beliefs with unparalleled intelligence, gentleness, and merriment
to generations of students."[4]

A Michigan native initially educated at the University of Michigan, Moore
went on to graduate school at Princeton University where he studied
with some of the most brilliant architects and educators of the nineteen-
fifties: Louis I. Kahn, Enrico Peressutti, Jean Labatut, and Donald Drew
Egbert.[5] Among the first graduates of Princeton's doctoral program in architecture, Moore completed a dissertation entitled "Water and Architecture"
in 1957, and was one of the few practicing architects of his generation to
hold a doctorate.[6]

After graduating from Princeton, Moore served as Kahn's teaching assis-
tant before being hired to teach at Berkeley. Once in San Francisco,
Moore formed an architectural partnership called Moore Lyndon Turnbull
Whitaker (MLTW), with fellow Princeton alumni Donlyn Lyndon and William
Turnbull (the fourth partner, Richard Whitaker, graduated from Berkeley).
During these years, Moore and MLTW articulated a position that combined
humanism—acknowledging both the individual agent and cultural mem-
ory—with environmental sensitivity, best expressed in the design of the
Sea Ranch Condominium of 1964–1965.

previous spread:
Photograph of Charles W.
Moore at Yale, ca. 1965.
above: Charles W. Moore in
the 1960s.

Named chairman at Yale in 1965, Moore may be seen as continuing the school's traditional emphasis on individual personality rather than ideology or theoretical program. Since its origins in the nineteenth century, the Yale School of Architecture has followed a unique path, different in many ways from most American architecture schools. Founded through a gift of Augustus Russell Street, the Yale School of Art opened in 1864 in Street Hall on Chapel Street.[7] Architectural instruction began in the School of Art in 1908, and was formalized into a department in 1923 as part of the newly named School of Fine Arts, which incorporated painting, sculpture, drama, and courses in the history of art. This contrasts with the more typical pattern in this country of establishing architectural programs as part of schools of engineering, such as at Massachusetts Institute of Technology (MIT) or the University of Michigan. Although organized along the lines of the École des Beaux-Arts in Paris, Yale's Department of Architecture never had a dominating Beaux-Arts-trained instructor, such as Paul Cret at the University of Pennsylvania or Jean Labatut at Princeton. Instead, it developed a visiting critic system in which teaching was tied to the personality of visiting critics and the chairman of the department.[8] This varied from the historicism of James Gamble Rogers's office to the early modernism of Raymond Hood and the international style of Wallace K. Harrison. Like all of the school's principal design critics—from Hood and Harrison through Edward Durell Stone, George Howe, Louis I. Kahn, Paul Schweikher, and Paul M. Rudolph—Moore was a practicing architect.

The differences between Moore and Rudolph, his immediate predecessor, outweigh similarities, however. Born in 1918 in Kentucky, Rudolph was educated at Alabama Polytechnic Institute (now Auburn University) and Harvard's Graduate School of Design. As chairman of Yale's Department of Architecture from 1958 to 1965, Rudolph had the most significant influence on the direction of the school in the post-war era, turning it into what was arguably the country's best architecture program.[9] Moore was nevertheless staunchly opposed to such late-modernist works as Rudolph's 1963 Art & Architecture Building at Yale, which he, in tandem with other critics of the nascent postmodern movement, considered an example of "exclusive" or univocal architecture, fortress-like in its invulnerability.[10] By contrast, Moore believed that architects should be vulnerable, and he embraced a commitment to artistic and social diversity best characterized under the rubric of "inclusiveness."[11]

Moore at Yale
Soon after his arrival in New Haven, Moore, bursting with ideas, made dramatic changes to the graduate curriculum. As Robert A.M. Stern later observed, under Moore's direction Yale's architecture program "swung from an emphasis on shape elaboration toward a concern for the usefulness of architecture in relation to the problems of life in our less advantaged areas, in our cities, and in our backwater locales."[12] In 1967, *Progressive Architecture* took note of how Moore introduced a new emphasis on the direct involvement of students in real-world problems:

> *Since the appointment of Charles W. Moore as chairman of the Department of Architecture at Yale, things have been taking on a decidedly non-Ivory Tower aspect. Not that such illustrious predecessors as Rudolph, Schweikher, and Howe were any slouches at leading and inspiring, but Moore's technique these days seems to be to get the students right out of the New Haven atmosphere and right down to the heady atmosphere of the client argument, the less-than-glamorous activities of figuring budgets and scheduling construction, and the hands-in-the-dirt experience of pouring foundations and putting up siding.[13]*

As part of his educational initiative, Moore hired several new faculty members, one of whom, Kent Bloomer, would prove particularly important to the innovations soon to follow. Bloomer was educated as an architect at MIT

before studying sculpture at Yale, where he received the MFA in 1961. Soon after graduating from Yale, Bloomer became a highly regarded instructor in the architecture department at Pittsburgh's Carnegie Institute of Technology (the precursor to Carnegie Mellon University), where he gained renown for an innovative course in basic design that was the much-admired center-piece of the first-year curriculum.[14] Derived from his studies with Bauhaus-trained Josef Albers at Yale and Gyorgy Kepes at MIT, Bloomer's course presented students with visual exercises on themes such as three-dimensional joint problems, or sculptures having dominant voids. Bloomer had his students build large models three to eight feet tall which transformed the studio by each semester's end.[15]

When Bloomer joined Moore in 1966 at Yale, they focused their efforts on revising the first-year curriculum in order to emphasize actual experience. In an article titled "Learning Under Moore," F. Andrus Burr, a member of the first class to undergo the new curriculum, described how the instructors "laid out a series of designing and 'making' exercises that concentrated on basic architectural questions: from how to join two materials together, to how people use a bathroom. Moore and Bloomer encouraged straightfor-ward, intuitive responses to these exercises. It was both an act of learning and a process of deprogramming—erasing the preconceptions."[16] Moore and Bloomer's educational philosophy was summarized in a statement of the goals of the department that first appeared in the January 1967 *Bulletin* of the architecture school:

> The architecture student, even if he has an extensive academic back-ground, must usually start from the beginning to see things and to understand the processes that give them their shape, and to communicate this understanding...A curious aspect of the outlook required of the architect, now as in the past, is the unembarrassed juxtaposition of concern for the closely finite, like doorknobs, with concerns for the most general concepts, like the extent and importance of the public realm in a democratic society.[17]

The themes announced here—the need for students to begin at the begin-ning, the importance of process, and the sense of responsibility to the public realm—stand in contrast to the description of the department that preceded Moore. Immediately before Moore's arrival, the *Bulletin* offered a dry yet succinct statement of the school's educational mission: "Training in the prac-tice of architecture is based on the concept that architecture is the rational integration of the art and the science of building."[18]

Moore and Bloomer encouraged students to get out of the studio in order to develop talents other than drafting ability.[19] According to Bloomer, Moore was opposed to students spending too much time in the drafting room if it led to sealing themselves off from actual experience.[20]

Significantly, Moore may not have initiated this focus on direct experi-ence and the turn away from the drafting room; rather, his own interests coincided with student-instigated trends and, in particular, on what could be called, for want of a better phrase, a design-build culture that already existed at Yale. This design-build culture was largely initiated by two members of the class of 1965, David E. Sellers and Peter L. Gluck.[21] In 1962, Sellers took time off from architecture school to design and build a house for his brother near Poughkeepsie, assisted on weekends by a few of his former classmates, such as Gluck, Etel Kramer, and M.J. Long.[22] In 1963, Sellers returned the favor to Gluck by helping him build a vacation house for Gluck's parents in Westhampton, New York. The cedar-clad house, supported on telephone poles, eventually took two sum-mers' worth of "filial labor" to build, and was featured in a 1967 article in *Progressive Architecture* that described the young Gluck as "plunging headlong into architecture—designing, building and developing."[23]

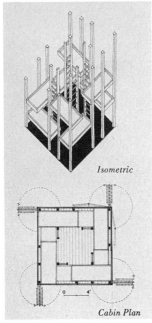

Isometric

Cabin Plan

top: Photograph by Hans Namuth of David Sellers and William Reinecke in front of the Pope House in "Prickly Mountain," Vermont.
bottom: Isometric and plan of the cabin at Camp Farnam, Connecticut, designed and built by Yale students in 1966.

After their graduation in 1965, Sellers and Gluck each purchased land in Vermont with the intention of building their own designs—a manifestation of the entrepreneurship that educator Denise Scott Brown has described as characteristic of Yale architecture students during the nineteen-sixties.[24] Gluck purchased 100 acres near Warren, Vermont, for which he designed vacation condominiums that were actually erected a few years later in a nearby town, Bolton.[25] Sellers purchased land near Sugarbush in the ski region along Mad River as the site for ski houses. With classmate William Reinecke, Sellers moved to the rural area to design and build these houses, both for themselves and to be sold on speculation, effectively establish- ing one of the country's first design-build architectural practices. Charles Hosford, along with Thomas Luckey and Louis Mackall, both of whom were still students, joined Sellers and Reinecke in Vermont, forming something of an architectural commune. In an article published in the May 1966 issue of *Progressive Architecture* about the ski cabins these young practitioners built for a development they called "Prickly Mountain," architectural journalist C. Ray Smith described their design-build process as "architec- tural happenings."[26] The twenty-six-year-old Sellers and Reinecke argued for "chance" and "indeterminacy," and saw the building process itself as "a source of inspiration." "This on-site improvisation," Smith wrote, "is an attempt to get beneath the veneer of the creative process, to seize the seeds of architectural ideas."[27]

Sellers and Reinecke eventually built over twenty houses; were written up in *Fortune* and *Life*; and were photographed by Hans Namuth for *House Beautiful.*[28] Their success inspired a growing enthusiasm at Yale for students trying their hands at building their own designs. This may be seen in a 1966 upper-level studio taught by Peter Millard and Paul Mitarachi with Felix Drury, a former Princeton classmate of Moore's, as a visiting critic.[29] The problem the instructors gave their third-year students was to design and build a cabin at Camp Farnam, a summer camp for underprivileged chil- dren in Durham, Connecticut. The selected design by William P. Hersey, a member of the class of 1967, was a compact, shed-roof cabin approximately 159 square feet in size containing built-in bunks for seven campers and one counselor in a spiral arrangement.[30] Glenn Gregg, a student in the stu- dio, recalls how he and his classmates began construction over the course of the 1966 spring break. "Long before the expertise that Paul Brouard would bring to the building project, we muddled our way through, pouring not- quite-vertical concrete piers for each corner that engineer Herman Spiegel swore never set—just froze in place, as we had begun in March—on a modestly sloping site," Gregg remembers.[31] The construction phase had its attendant benefits as a social experience: "As we labored through the break," Gregg recalls, "we got to know our fellow classmates in a way that no amount of socializing in the studio could ever offer."[32]

The First-Year Building Project

Moore seized on these initiatives and directed them in a socially respon- sive direction. The Vermont cabins built by Sellers and his peers were individual, private houses built for profit. One, the Pope House, was for a Wall Street broker. By contrast, the first building project Moore organized was for a community center in one of the poorest areas of the country, Appalachia. "Of all the memories of Yale, the Building Program is the stron- gest, and, for me, the one that I am most proud of," Moore later confided.[33] In a 1968 article, Moore described the intentions that led to the creation of the First-Year Building Project:

> *I believe that architecture is only properly teachable in terms of use in response to the people who are to inhabit buildings, their life styles, their concerns, their privacy, and their public realm. To teach architecture simply as the composition of shapes is out of the question. Yet for the designer to be able to operate at all, he must be able to make things*

top: Photograph of Yale students at Camp Farnam in Durham, Connecticut, ca. 1966.
middle: Photograph of boathouse in Jackson County, Kentucky, ca. 1966, designed and built by Tom Carey and Steve Edwins.
bottom: Photograph of Yale students with Charles W. Moore and Kent Bloomer in Jackson County, Kentucky, 1967.

knowingly, to compose shapes and voids, as well as to manipulate programmatic firsts. [34]

Moore had taken note of the rising concern of students "to make design more responsive to the complex needs of the world around us."[35] The primary intention of the Yale Building Project was educational. Direct experience—working as teams on the design for a real client, and then seeing the final design through the whole process of building—was a way to get students away from purely academic "paper architecture," and to harness their desire to engage social issues. Moore may also be seen to have reined in the overtly individualistic qualities of Sellers and his peers, and their devotion to free enterprise, by having the first-year students work together in teams on a community center.

The conception of the Building Project responded to calls for "relevance" in the culture of the 1960s.[36] Tom Carey, a member of the class of 1970, recalls that students were restless and impatient: "They wanted to do more than draw buildings that would never happen."[37] Moore and Bloomer established a process in which student input was a vital component. Moore described how:

> *Students helped establish a number of criteria from the beginning for the building we would do. First, it had to matter. Whatever it was, it had substantially to change the lives of people who used it. Second, because of the enthusiasms of students then, any building had to be for poor people. And third, as a practical matter, it had to be of a size that was buildable within the time available to us. We took it that larger problems, ones which were probably not solvable by building alone or on which building might not even make an applicable dent—as, for instance, the problems of Harlem—were inappropriate to the first year. Instead, the real problems of a small community we might work with—like a rural community in Appalachia—were more appropriate to our capacity and concerns.* [38]

The passage reveals the combination of socially progressive goals with pragmatic thinking that was essential to the success of the educational objective.

It was, in fact, three students—Tom Carey, Steve Edwins, and Robert Swenson, all of whom were originally members of the class of 1969, who found the project the class would work on. Swenson was the first to travel to Appalachia, where he helped in politically organizing impoverished residents of Kentucky's Perry County during the summer of 1964 when he was a college student at Southern Illinois University. Once in graduate school at Yale, Swenson made his classmates aware of a Catholic volunteer organization called the Christian Appalachian Project (C.A.P.), founded in 1964 by a charismatic priest, Father Ralph Beiting. Interested in the work of Father Beiting, Carey and Edwins spent the summer of 1966 in Jackson County, Kentucky, joined briefly by Swenson, to work on a children's camp run by C.A.P. Carey recalls how he lived in a trailer, received free room and board, and was paid $1.00 a day to design and help build a boathouse for the camp.[39] Carey took a leave of absence from Yale for the 1966–1967 academic year to stay in Kentucky, where he designed and built a small house for a poor miner and his family in the town of Millstone.

Inspired by the work of Carey, Edwins, and Swenson, several of their classmates, now in their second year at Yale, formed a group they called Group Nine, in association with their design studio instructor Pat Goeters, and looked for ways to become involved with low-income communities in eastern Kentucky. In addition to Carey and Swenson, Group Nine included Peter Hentschel, Dave Hoeffner, Robert Kurzon, William Richardson, Paul Thompson, and Robert White.[40] During the fall 1966 semester, these students drove to eastern Kentucky and lived at a settlement school in the

top: Photograph of Yale
students in Jackson County,
Kentucky, 1967.

town of Hindman in Knox County. They met with local community organizers
and with prominent residents of the town of Whitesburg, such as the writer
Harry Caudill, and Tom and Pat Gish, publishers of the *Whitesburg Mountain
Eagle*. Supported by Moore, the students found a project to work on for
the remainder of the 1966–1967 academic year: preparing a site plan for
approximately twenty new houses for families who were to be relocated
as a result of the construction of the Carr Fork Dam by the Army Corps of
Engineers in southern Knox County.[41]

The interest among college and university students of this era in Appalachia
was a reflection of the Great Society of Lyndon Johnson, an ambitious
initiative of social betterment, which the president announced in a 1964
commencement speech at the University of Michigan. Earlier that year,
Johnson had declared an "unconditional war on poverty," and proposed
the Economic Opportunity Act as the centerpiece of an effort to eradicate
deprivation in America.[42] Passed by the Congress in August 1964, the Act
created several programs, such as the Office of Economic Opportunity,
the VISTA program (Volunteers in Service to America), the Job Corps, the
Neighborhood Youth Corps, and what were called "Community Action"
efforts.[43] Led by Sargent Shriver, the founding director of the Peace Corps
during the presidency of John F. Kennedy, these programs focused on areas
of entrenched poverty such as Appalachia, which Johnson had toured in
1960 as Kennedy's running mate, and then again in 1964 as president. As
Harry Caudill recounts in his 1976 book, *The Watches of the Night*, students
from elite universities took such an interest in the problems of Appalachia
that they created a near-invasion of the region during the second half of the
nineteen-sixties.[44]

Caudill's comment may be dyspeptic; nevertheless, it is true that less than
four years after its founding, VISTA received more applications from
college students than the Peace Corps did, as young people turned toward
America's internal problems. One notable initiative in this regard was the
Appalachian Volunteers, a group of college-age youth who, beginning in
1964, undertook to paint and repair dilapidated one- and two-room school-
houses in remote areas of eastern Kentucky, southwestern Virginia, West
Virginia, and Tennessee. Their efforts later encompassed tutoring, roadbuilding, improving sanitation, and political activism. The Harvard psycholo-
gist Robert Coles studied the Appalachian Volunteers as an example of how
"American youth have shown themselves capable of exceptionally vigorous
participation" in civic life.[45]

Moore visited the Yale students who were working in Kentucky in 1966,
during which time he became friends with Father Beiting, the director of
C.A.P., and renewed his acquaintance with Charles Graves, the dean at
the School of Architecture at the University of Kentucky. Beiting made the
Yale students in Kentucky aware of two local groups in Appalachia that
needed buildings. One project was for low-income housing in eastern
Kentucky, and the other was a community center for a town called New Zion
in Jackson County, in the east central part of the state.

New Zion was a rural community located near the town of McKee, about
seventy miles southeast of Lexington. F. Andrus Burr described it as "a
tiny town in the Appalachian Mountains ... a genuine backwoods town with
no local government and not one flush toilet among two hundred inhabitants."[46] Class member Alberto Lau characterized it as "a scattering of
farmhouses grouped under a common name" located in one of the poorest
regions in the state.[47] William Richardson remembers the shock of his
initial trip to the region, when he drove on rutted dirt roads through the
hollers among flimsy wood shacks with wallpaper for insulation, and
saw men shooting squirrels for dinner. As Carey noted, "It was a totally
different world" for these young students from an East Coast school.[48]

top: Cover of the May 1966 issue of *Progressive Architecture* showing the Sea Ranch Condominium in Gualala, California, designed by MLTW. middle: Exterior photograph of the New Zion Community Center. bottom: Exterior photograph of the New Zion Community Center, 1967.

After developing relationships with community organizers in New Zion that would prove essential to the involvement of Yale, Carey stayed in eastern Kentucky to work on the C.A.P. housing project. Edwins and Swenson then presented the proposed community center in New Zion as a possible extracurricular project in a conversation with chairman Moore. Edwins remembers Moore as open to suggestions by students and willing to let people try things out. Moore decided that he would make the community center the design project for the spring 1967 semester of the first-year class and that he would teach the studio, along with Bloomer and four other faculty: Herbert Newman, Paul Helmle, Herman Spiegel, and Luis Summers.[49] Early in the spring 1967 semester, Moore asked the second-year students in Group Nine, now back in New Haven, to make a presentation to the first-year class about their experiences in Kentucky.[50]

After agreeing to the project, the thirty first-year students divided themselves into six design groups ranging in size from four to nine members. Each group gave themselves a name, most of which were based on the construction system they proposed; for example, "Stud and Skin" used a balloon frame in their design, and "Land Formation" incorporated sculptured earth in their proposal.[51] The student teams arrived at their designs following consultations with the New Zion Community Association, an organization composed of approximately twenty-four families that had purchased a half-acre of land for the center. Small delegations of students traveled to rural Kentucky to elicit the community's needs for their new center. A program was identified that called for a large multipurpose room, a meeting room, a library, and ancillary service spaces—kitchen, toilets, shower, and storage. The multipurpose room would be used primarily for meetings and basketball, and less often as a dance floor and dining room. Important to the commission was the fact that the building was to be a focal point for the community's young people. Families hoped to stem the tide of youth leaving the region.[52]

At the conclusion of the design phase, each of the student teams presented their proposal to the class as a whole. First the faculty, then the class, voted on the one to be built.[53] The team that called itself "Group-Group" was the winner. It numbered eight: Alberto Lau, Tom Dryer, Peter Rose, Peter Woerner (all of whom had attended Yale College), Andy Burr, Walter "Budge" Upton, Jerry Wagner (graduates of Williams College), and Tom Platt (a graduate of Colgate).

Lau described how "faculty involvement during the design process was mainly through criticism; the construction phase was totally student-run."[54] Peter Woerner devised a critical path analysis that was used in scheduling both the drawing phase and the construction timetable; Moore later saluted the "astonishing accuracy and usefulness" of Woerner's work.[55] During the 1967 spring vacation, the entire class traveled to Kentucky to build the project. Some of the students lived with local families while others camped in the hamlet's one-room schoolhouse. Burr conveyed the risks of the enterprise when he described how "the Building Project was unprecedented in architectural education, and the idea was replete with potential disasters." Once on site, Burr felt the magnitude of the challenge he and his classmates faced. "The class arrived in Kentucky with a vague design and many uncertainties," he wrote. "The extreme rural conditions meant that there were no subcontractors available, and so the Yalies had to do all the work themselves: hand-digging the foundations and septic field, installing the plumbing and wiring, and building the structure." Nevertheless, "stimulated by adversity, many talents emerged."[56]

The Community Center at New Zion
The final design was an almost-square building, in which the large, rectangular "multipurpose room" opened off a series of tightly organized service spaces, which included an entry porch; a vestibule with a staircase to a

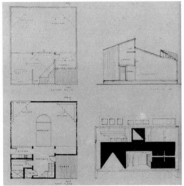

top: Interior photograph of
the New Zion Community
Center.
bottom: Plans, section, and
cut-away perspective of
the New Zion Community
Center.

second floor; and the requested kitchen, storage, and toilet with shower. The clarity of organization into service and served zones reflected the influence of Louis I. Kahn who, although no longer on the Yale faculty, continued to be admired by Yale students. The 1965 issue of *Perspecta*, for example, had devoted thirty-three pages to Kahn's work. The common room was two stories tall at its highest point beneath the sloping roof, and large enough to accommodate half a basketball court. The partial second floor contained a library and a small meeting room on either side of the staircase hall, with balconies that overlooked the multipurpose room.

The design idiom was the "shed" style of the mid 1960s, the major precedent being the Sea Ranch Condominium in Gualala, California, by Moore and his firm, MLTW. The redwood-sided Sea Ranch was widely published in architectural journals after its completion in 1965.[57] Burr, for example, described "how stunningly new and exciting the condominium was in 1965."[58] Its sloping roof is echoed at the New Zion Community Center, the exterior of which was sheathed in unpainted vertical oak siding. The use of wood at New Zion related to neighboring houses, while the building's sharp-edged forms clearly identified it as a special, designed artifact.

The main architectural gestures on the exterior were triangular "pop-ups" for the clerestory windows, and a large, orange-painted barn door on exterior tracks. According to Lau, this large opening gave access to a spectacular view and provided cross-ventilation during the summer.[59] It also allowed local farmers to load their produce in an accessible spot, in an effort to induce trucking companies to stop and pick up their crops.[60] Seemingly simple and functional, the barn door was also a sophisticated design element. From the outside, the door endowed the building with a large scale that identified it as a public, rather than domestic, structure, and its location at the extreme corner allowed daylight to rake the perpendicular wall. This type of large opening placed at the extreme corners of compact buildings was a design device Moore himself favored, such as at his house in Orinda, California. Moore, Gerald Allen, and Donald Lyndon would later include a diagram of this lighting effect in their 1974 book, *The Place of Houses.*

The students were inventive in introducing light into the interior of the community center: at the two outer corners of the common room, for example, the triangular "pop-ups" had both clerestory windows and translucent skylights made from corrugated fiberglass that provided indirect light. Most likely based on Moore's use of fiberglass on the shed roofs of the 1966 Sea Ranch Athletic Cub, a similar skylight above the staircase permitted light to filter down into the vestibule of the community center.

The interior perimeter walls of the multipurpose room were left unfinished. One strong design on the interior was the use of bold cut-out shapes on the partition dividing the kitchen, vestibule, and closet from the multipurpose room. Lau described this partition as "a wall full of goodies with a basketball ring on it, small spaces with a variety of functions behind it, and light streaming from the triangular skylight at the top."[61] Moore used similar large, cut-out shapes in the wood-framed house on Elm Street in New Haven that he renovated while teaching at Yale. (Students helped build this renovation, which was an ongoing building project in itself.)

The New Zion building had a distinctive presence. Sympathetic to both neighboring buildings and its natural setting, the center was nevertheless an accomplished design. In an interview with the editors of *Progressive Architecture*, Moore declared it "an extraordinarily handsome structure, with sophisticated shapes that admit light artfully."[62] Moore thought that the students were especially successful in designing for the youth of the community. He described the center as "not only a place to play marbles or basketball or whatever, it is—in the best and most useful sense—itself a toy."[63]

19

Important to Moore was not just the finished product, however skillful as a design, but the process that the students and community members went through. He described how the building was the result of a process

> ...that has brought about a complicated and powerful set of involvements of class members with the citizens of New Zion, as they worried together about the site and hammered out a program, and as the New Zionists accepted them into their midst; and of class members with each other, as they planned the building, and overcame each others' resistances, as they organized to build it, and then as they built it together, very quickly.[64]

The passage reveals Moore's understanding of the importance of collaboration and social involvement in architectural education. He stated that a visitor to the site during construction "delighted me by noting with astonishment that he had not heard anybody in the class say 'I'; everybody kept talking about what 'we' were doing."[65] The optimism of this period in American culture, which preceded a later cynicism induced by events such as the prolongation of the conflict in Vietnam and the Watergate break-in, finds expression in Moore's observations here.

Central to the experience was the interaction between Yale students and Appalachians, an interaction that engaged the skills and resources of both groups. Women from the community cooked for the student workers, preparing a lunch buffet each day during construction. Class member Daniel V. Scully recalls the "generous hospitality from those without much means but a sweetness of heart, and great cooking."[66] Thrilled that members of the community expressed their gratitude, Lau recalled, "As a resident of New Zion said: 'What's important is that you boys said you would do it, and did it.'"[67] In 1968, Moore acknowledged the generally positive response of the New Zion community, and suggested why they seemed to embrace the students' work, despite the newness of the design:

> [B]ecause it was built by people that the members of the community liked and enjoyed having among themselves, because it used some of the efforts of the members of the community itself, [the building] is apparently regarded not as some alien intrusion, or as something some Martians from Yale left behind, but as a useful facility which is a part of New Zion.[68]

What Did the Students Learn?
Moving beyond intentions, what did the students learn? Class member Lau described the experience in the September 1967 cover article in *Progressive Architecture*. The fact that *Progressive Architecture* devoted its cover to the project indicates that the editors acknowledged the magnitude of the achievement. Lau stated that "the educational value of the building was very great, more than any other project done in school."[69] He described what lessons he and his classmates learned when he wrote:

> We learned a lot through coming into direct contact with construction. Design decisions were made with the consideration in mind that this building was to be built by the class, not by master carpenters, with a limited budget. ... Living with families in New Zion was also a great experience. We came to understand their way of life and their way of thinking. The community center will have value if it can be adapted to their living, and hopefully, if it is capable of changing their way of life, in some small way, for the better.[70]

It is important to note the students' belief that architecture could change people's lives. This modest, but genuine, activism may be the best expression of Moore's pedagogic influence. It reflects the humanism of Moore's teaching and the idealism of Lau's generation. The role of motivated, resourceful students having both social consciences and

top: Photograph of Kent
Bloomer with Ellen Leopold,
Stephen Douglas, Mark Ellis,
David Hager, and David
Shepler, 1968.
bottom: Exterior photo-
graph of the Lower Grassy-
Trace Branch Community
Center in Leslie County,
Kentucky, 1968.

entrepreneurial skills must be underscored. Moore credited his students for their sense of social responsibility: "The morality of bright students in the '60s is certainly a morality of involvement," he told the editors of *Progressive Architecture*.[71]

The experience changed the lives of many of the students, as Burr remarked: "After eight delirious weeks, first-year had a building, not to mention a pleasant feeling of satisfaction and self-confidence."[72] According to Burr, the building project gave the students a "unique identity" and sense of empowerment: "the affirming and energizing experience of making one's own building." Sounding a similar note, Robert Stern later wrote, "For young architects, the first lesson of New Zion, which Moore had really begun to teach in the early 1960s, was one of exhilarating power. They didn't have to be old and hoary to build; they could make things now."[73] As architect and educator Denise Scott Brown observed in a different context, "It's good to learn together, and lessons learned with comrades in adversity sear you for life."[74]

These were the lessons learned by succeeding generations of Yale students. Contacts made in rural Kentucky during the planning and building of the New Zion Community Center led to the building project for the next year's entering class. This was also a community center—now for the inhabitants of two settlements along creek banks called Lower Grassy and Trace Branch located in Leslie County, about fifty miles southeast of New Zion. Members of this community had observed the Yale students construct the community center in New Zion, and a local organization called the Lower Grassy-Trace Branch Community Development Organization contacted Moore at Yale directly, once funding from the U.S. Department of Housing and Urban Development was assured.[75]

The Community Center in Lower Grassy

The process used in the first building project was followed at Lower Grassy with a similarly successful result. Students traveled between New Haven and Appalachia, where they met with local representatives. The class divided themselves into design teams, and after a competition to select a final design, the entire class moved to Kentucky to construct the building. The winning design team was composed of five students: Stephen Douglas, Mark Ellis, David Hager, Ellen Leopold, and David Shepler.[76] The program was more complex than its predecessor, since the Lower Grassy families asked for additional spaces, such as a clinic for a visiting nurse, an office with a phone for a VISTA worker, and a classroom where high school students could study (as most homes were badly overcrowded).[77] The site at Lower Grassy was on a steep hill located off the main road leading out of one of the county's largest towns, Hyden. The angular, "active" forms of the design responded to this prominent position in the landscape, and its four interior levels accommodated the building's sloping site.

Mark Ellis, a member of the design team, described the process in an article published in the December 1968 issue of *Interiors* magazine. This may seem like an unlikely venue for an article on a low-budget, socially responsible building for the impoverished, but it points to both the ability of Yale students to publicize their efforts, and a receptiveness to innovative work that existed in the design culture of the time. Ellis wrote:

> *Yale's Department of Architecture was among the first in this country to recognize the advantages of confronting the students not only with hypothetical problems, but real design projects to carry through all stages of construction—giving the student a taste of client relations, a feel for human scale, and experiences of actual construction practices. Almost the entire first-year design class (of about 30) took two weeks in May to visit Lower Grassy, living and eating with families on the creek, attending community meetings, and learning how to pour concrete and lay cinder block. Working day and night (under floodlights stolen from the Drama School),*

21

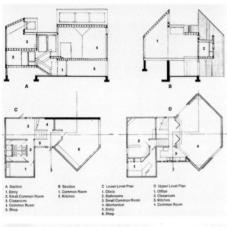

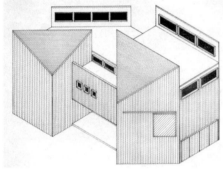

top: Exterior photograph of the Lower Grassy-Trace Branch Community Center, 1968.
middle: Sections and plans of the Lower Grassy-Trace Branch Community Center, 1968.
bottom: Isometric drawing of the Lower Grassy-Trace Branch Community Center, 1968.

we had the foundation complete at the end of two weeks, and were finished with concrete work and into rough framing.[78]

As the building took shape, community members expressed satisfaction that "something is actually happening after three years of talk." While most of the class stayed just two weeks in early May, living with local families, a crew of four students returned in the summer to complete most of the building. Besides Ellis, they included Robert Hammell, Robert Nicolais, and David Shepler. Assisted during the summer by Neighborhood Youth Corps boys, they eventually returned to New Haven for the beginning of classes in the fall. The building was useable by December 1968, although completion of the interior finishes continued into the early months of 1969.

Like his predecessors in the class of 1970, Ellis remarked on the sense of satisfaction and personal growth that the experience offered. He wrote:

We enjoy the feeling that we have participated constructively in the life of the inhabitants of this timeless region, where people farm the hills for subsistence in much the same way as their ancestors learned from the Indians. By personally handling the entire construction—from dealings with the government and keeping our creditors at bay through actual carpentry—we may have learned even more than our school expected.[79]

Ellis's classmate and fellow design team member Ellen Leopold described the project as "without doubt, the best part of my experience at Yale."[80] For Leopold, this experience also contributed to her political education, as she gained firsthand experience of a part of America she previously never knew. Important to Leopold in this regard was reading Harry Caudill's evocative history of the region, *Night Comes to the Cumberlands.*

The Innovative Nature of the Program
The First-Year Building Project was an innovation in educating architects in America, embodying a clear, even revolutionary, rejection of the Beaux-Arts studio system that still prevailed, despite attempts at reform by modernists such as Walter Gropius at Harvard and Mies van der Rohe at Illinois Institute of Technology. While many schools had modernized their curricula, the fundamental structure of architectural education remained the same. As Moore noted in 1967, "the Beaux-Arts method persisted in most schools, surprisingly unchanged."[81] In architectural education modeled on the academic system of the École des Beaux-Arts, students devoted their energies to carefully rendered—indeed lavish—drawings of projects that were usually of cultural prominence or national significance, such as libraries, museums, or halls of justice. It was a hierarchically organized system, with the head of each atelier at the top of a pyramid descending downward to neophyte students. Denise Scott Brown has described it as a "hierarchic culture of students divided into *anciens, aspirants,* and *nouveaux,* presided over by the stern, stiff *patron.*"[82]

The very concept of designing and actually building a center intended for the youth of a poor, rural community was a significant break with the Beaux-Arts legacy. In an overview of the programs for Grand Prix competitions in the 265-year history of the École, for example, historian Donald Drew Egbert observed that "programs of buildings for commoners have been extremely rare, [as] have programs of primarily humanitarian or sociological connotation."[83] While retaining the design competition that was at the heart of the Beaux-Arts model, the First-Year Building Project shifted the locus of the architectural student's identification from the *atelier* to the *chantier,* proposing a more engaged definition of the architect.

Precedents for the program further back in time than the efforts of the Prickly Mountain entourage or the work of the Appalachian volunteers are difficult to discern. There is the example of John Ruskin, who, as Slade

Photographs of Yale students building the Lower Grassy-Trace Branch Community Center, 1968.

Professor of Fine Arts at Oxford University, enjoined undergraduates to help him build a road in a swampy area of Ferry Hinksey southwest of Oxford, England, in 1874–1875.[84] Intended to unite the practical to the ethical, the roadbuilding endeavor extended over several terms, and was part of Ruskin's larger commitment to social improvement.

Closer to home, there may have been a precedent in 1952 when polymath R. Buckminster Fuller taught at Yale, leading sixty-two students, drawn from the Departments of Architecture and Art, to construct a geodesic dome on campus.[85] Thirty feet in diameter, made of cardboard and tape, the dome was placed on the roof of one of the towers of Weir Hall, where some of the studios of the Department of Architecture were housed. Vincent Scully described the event in lighthearted terms, noting that the cardboard dome "built by dazed students ... rotted impressively for some time."[86] The exercise had none of the socially responsible imperatives of the Yale Building Project developed under Moore, but the can-do optimism of Fuller and his injunctions to architects to become leaders in society may have laid the groundwork for later students' receptiveness to collaboration and learning by doing.

The teaching of Vincent Scully during this era should also be mentioned as an example of active engagement and as an expression of social responsibility. Scully's *American Architecture and Urbanism*, written in the late sixties and published in 1969, explicitly articulated a socially activist treatment of its subject. In its preface, for example, Scully reminded the reader that "his vote and his direct personal intervention in his own community can help determine the kind of world we will make."[87] Furthermore, in 1951, Scully had designed his own family's house in Woodbridge, Connecticut, which, while not an example of design-build, remains a rare example of engagement with the act of building by an architectural historian.[88]

The Program As Catalyst

Yale's First-Year Building Project at once reflected larger cultural currents and served as a catalyst in the design culture of the time. Important to this was the deftness with which Yale students arranged to have themselves and their work photographed and discussed in the media. Ellis's article in *Interiors* on the Lower Grassy-Trace Branch Community Center, for example, was generously accompanied by eight pages of photographs of the building taking shape and of the students themselves at work. When *Progressive Architecture* placed the New Zion Community Center on the cover of its September 1967 issue, it brought enormous attention to the first efforts of this educational initiative.[89] Indeed, during the following years, *Progressive Architecture* came to be dubbed "the Yale Alumni Magazine" since it devoted so many articles to the work of Elis and to events at the school.[90] A good deal of this attention certainly devolved from Moore, who, as David Littlejohn has noted, attracted more notice in architectural publications than any other American architect during the late 1960s and early 1970s.[91]

An important figure in this focus on Yale was architectural journalist C. Ray Smith, who, after attending Kenyon College in Ohio, received a master of arts degree in English from Yale. During the eight-year period in which he was an associate editor at *Progressive Architecture*, Smith published fifty-seven articles, most of which featured Yale-trained architects, such as the Prickly Mountain group (Sellers, Reinecke, Mackall, Hosford, and Luckey), Doug Michels (co-founder of the architectural collective Ant Farm), or faculty members connected with Yale, such as Rudolph, Moore, and Robert Venturi. During the period from 1965 to 1968, "young architecture students," according to Smith, "created a flash fire of social and optical activity that came to the profession's attention, even before their graduation."[92] Most of these were Yale students.

The well-publicized success of the First-Year Building Project, combined with the continuing influence of Yale graduates Sellers and Reinecke, made

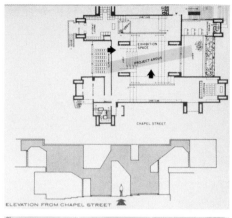

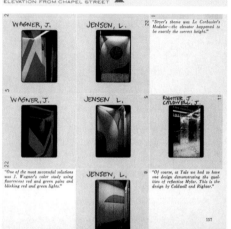

top: Diagrammatic plan and
section of Project Argus,
ca. 1968.
bottom: Designs by Yale
students for alterations to
the elevator cabs in the Art
& Architecture Building,
ca. 1968.

Yale the focus for design-build activities during the late 1960s and early 1970s.[93] Many of these efforts took place at small schools in the northeast, which had progressive or experimental components as part of their educational missions. For example, in 1966–1967, about ninety students at the Putney School, a preparatory school in rural Vermont, contributed manual labor in the construction of a new dormitory designed by architect John B. Rogers of the firm Homer-Rogers. The building took two years to build and was conceived, in part, as a learning exercise for students.[94] In the spring of 1967, Franconia College, a small experimental college in the White Mountain region of New Hampshire, hired a recent graduate of the University of Pennsylvania, Edward D'Andrea, to organize a design-build experience for its students. D'Andrea has described how he and his peers were inspired by Sellers's work at Prickly Mountain: "It suddenly occurred to students that they were going to be architects someday, and that they could already build buildings."[95] Working with a young landscape designer, D'Andrea sketched out rough plans for a dormitory for twenty students, who would actually construct the building. The students and designers spent one summer and the following fall semester building the five-story, 6,000-square-foot building; the students then proceeded to design and finish their own rooms in conjunction with an interior design course. The wood sheathing and angled geometry of the dormitory bear similarities to Sellers's and Reinecke's Tack House, and the designers' emphasis on process reflects similar statements by the Prickly Mountain architects.

On a much smaller scale in the spring of 1967, architecture students at the Massachusetts of Technology subdivided their design studio with a few partitions and constructed mezzanines out of heavy timbers resting on concrete blocks, after which they encountered hostility from the MIT administration. The following fall, however, Donlyn Lyndon, Moore's former student at Princeton and a partner of MLTW, took over as head of the department and allowed students to further subdivide and personalize the university's single-room architectural studio. For C. Ray Smith, such episodes were characteristic of the era's challenges to institutional structures.[96] One of the MIT students remarked on his "frustration of going through four years of drawing projects, and not building them," and it may be that some of this frustration was due, in part, at having read about Yale students' well-publicized successes in constructing an entire building with full institutional support.[97] There were a few similar episodes at other schools, where students constructed alterations to their studios, e.g., at the University of Houston under the direction of Howard Barnstone (a Yale graduate), and at the University of Texas at Austin under the direction of Richard Oliver (who had studied with Moore at Berkeley). It was at Yale, however, that the most numerous forays into education in which students built their own designs took place.

This may be seen in six projects from the years 1967–1969: Project Argus, a multimedia sculpture installed in the Art & Architecture Building; the temporary alteration of the elevator cabs in the same building; cabins for the Fresh Air Fund near Fishkill, New York; three foam houses constructed near the Yale golf course; a temporary marquee and pipe structure for the Yale School of Drama; and an arts and crafts building at a children's camp outside New Haven. It is remarkable how much actual building Yale architecture students undertook, particularly in 1968. Described by historians alternatively as America's *annus horribilis* or the year of protest, 1968 was for most architecture students at Yale a year in which they built their own designs, or in one case that of their instructors.[98]

Designed by Moore, Bloomer, and Drury, and constructed by students, Project Argus was a bridge-like structure that spanned the double-height exhibition space on the second floor of Rudolph's building. It was part of a temporary installation by a group of sculptors called Pulsa, who lined the walls of Project Argus with fluorescent lights that were activated by a synthesizer. Described as a "panoptic, multi-faceted sensory extrava-ganza" intended to "provide an open-ended experimental atmosphere," and sheathed in reflective mylar, Project Argus may have been influenced by Andy Warhol's silver-lined studio in New York.[99] It acted as a something of a rebuke to Rudolph's building, as it inserted a dynamic statement of Moore's principles of inclusiveness and multiple cultural references into Rudolph's cavernous central volume. The editors of *Progressive Architecture* understood this rebuke, describing how Project Argus "inflict[s] a dazzling bombard-ment" on Rudolph's building.[100] In an article in *The New York Times*—point-edly entitled "Kicked a Building Lately?"—architectural critic Ada Louise Huxtable saw in Project Argus the definitive sign of the waning of Rudolph's reputation, and the statement of a rising new generation. Huxtable wrote:

> *Yale architecture students agitated until their notably Supermannerist Dean, Charles Moore, aided in the destruction of one of the major areas of Paul Rudolph's Art & Architecture Building. They installed a pulsating white light, display of fluorescent tubing and silver mylar for a space [sic] and mind-bending esthetic experiment and design* double entendre *that practically told Mr. Rudolph to get up on the shelf and stay there.*[101]

Another critique of Rudolph's original design may be detected, to a lesser extent, in the temporary alteration of the interiors of the building's two elevator cabs, designed and implemented by Yale students during the 1968–1969 academic year. Graphic designer Barbara Stauffacher, who had designed supergraphics for the health club at MLTW's Sea Ranch Condominium, was hired by Moore as a visiting critic.[102] Stauffacher asked her students to modify and enliven the existing elevator cabs, which she described as drab. Students were required to present their schemes in model form. Fourteen of them, realized in paint alone, were selected for installation by the students on a rotating schedule.[103] *Progressive Architecture* published ten of the schemes in a full-color, double-page spread. Huxtable also published photographs of two of the student designs in *The New York Times*, and saluted the students' work "as legitimate exploratory exercises." She concluded her review by observing:

> *What is really happening is that the upcoming generation, full of beans, talent, revolt, and defensible disrespect for the tasteful totems and the huge hack symbols of the Establishment, is giving them a highly creative raspberry. You could call it a productive protest.*[104]

Huxtable's final line should be read in the context of its publication early in 1969, when many Americans were still reeling from the student protests and rebellions that rocked campuses throughout the course of the previous year. While this is not the place to discuss the social ramifications of these events, which have been extensively written about, it is relevant to note the concern that some of these protests had destructive aspects.[105] Huxtable's emphasis on the "productive protest" by the Yale students echoed the editorial comments that framed the article in *Interiors* on the building of the Lower Grassy-Trace Branch Community Center. The editors explained that they selected the Yale building project for such extensive coverage, since it "demonstrates the existence of "non-Yippies": youth concerned with the problems of our time, and working to solve them."[106]

A similar social imperative may be seen in a project that occurred during the summer of 1968, when a small group of first-year students designed and built cabins for the Fresh Air Fund. Founded in 1877, the Fund maintains a sleep-away camp for underprivileged children near Fishkill, New York, called Camp Hayden-Marks. After contributing to the construction of the community center for Lower Grassy and Trace Branch during the spring semester, ten members of the class of 1971 lived during the summer of 1968 in a farmhouse near Camp Hayden-Marks where they constructed several cabins in conjunction with the associate executive director of the Fund,

top: Exterior photograph of a dormitory cabin at Camp Hayden-Marks, Fishkill, New York, ca 1968.
second: Interior photograph of a dormitory cabin at Camp Hayden-Marks, Fishkill, New York, ca. 1968.
third: Exterior photograph of foam house, designed and built by Yale students in 1968.
bottom: Exterior photograph of foam house, designed and built by Yale students in 1968.

Laurence Mickolic, and a local carpenter. One innovative design by Ellen Leopold was for a cabin that stepped down a hillside, with each bunk bed on a separate level. Interviewed by *The New York Times* on the project, Kent Bloomer observed that "today's students have deep humanitarian feelings, so naturally this is a labor of love."[107]

In 1968, Felix Drury taught the spring design studio for the second-year class, who divided themselves into three teams, each of which designed and constructed a house made of spray-on foam. The project derived from Drury's interest in experimental materials, dating from the years he taught at Carnegie Institute of Technology, and from the research of a student in Yale's Master of Environmental Design Program, Valerie Batorewicz. Constructed near the Yale golf course during the summer of 1968, the houses were formed of polyurethane foam donated by the Union Carbide Corporation sprayed over inflated balloons covered in burlap.[108] For a free spirit like Drury, one of the attractions of foam construction was "to get away from the stick mentality," or wood-frame construction, in favor of experimental structures. Although Moore was interested in creative experimentation, he remained committed to conventional means of construction. Drury went on to organize over ten more foam houses during the following years.[109]

It was also in 1968 that the second-year class had a design competition for a combined marquee and pipe structure to be built in front of the Yale University Theater, home to the School of Drama, intended to highlight the presence of the building on York Street. The selected scheme, by Daniel V. Scully, consisted of an angular assemblage of steel pipes, illuminated by strings of lights, with two columnar kiosks fabricated from oil drums.[110] Led by Scully's classmate, Robert Knight, whose welding skills earned him the nickname "Torch," students built the temporary structure during the summer of 1968. Robert Brustein, dean of the School of Drama, described the assemblage as "in the spirit of the times in its protest against the Gothic façade of the School."[111] The structure served as a backdrop for one of the most infamous events at the school—the 1968 visit by the Living Theatre of Julian Beck and Judith Malina for a performance of *Paradise Now*. At the conclusion of the opening night performance, some members of the cast and audience were arrested for indecent exposure after partially disrobing in a bacchic celebration of the power of theater.[112]

More long-lasting was another project in 1968 by the second-year class: an arts and crafts building for Camp Cedarcrest in Orange, Connecticut. Located in a wooded area just beyond the New Haven city limits, Camp Cedarcrest has offered recreation to children from greater New Haven since 1924. Michael Curtis was lead designer for the selected scheme, a wood-sheathed, U-shaped building with large light monitors and diagonal walls that suggests the early work of architect Robert Venturi, such as his 1959 design for a beach house in New Jersey.[113] The interior of the arts and crafts building, which is still in use, is focused on a large brick fireplace, constructed by Daniel Scully and Roc Caivano during the summer of 1968. Caivano would find his experience as a brick mason useful when he later worked as an architect for Venturi, Scott Brown and Associates, known for their buildings with brick façades in complex patterns. Caivano recently reflected on his 1968 experience in a passage echoed by numerous architects who studied under Moore at Yale:

Those Yale building projects were wonderful. They helped us focus our enthusiasm and creativity; help other people; and enter the adult, professional world with confidence and delight.[114]

Conclusion: The Yale Building Project as Political Action

Fundamental to the educational objectives of the Yale Building Project developed by Moore was political engagement. I use the word "political" in the same sense that the French literary and cultural critic Roland Barthes

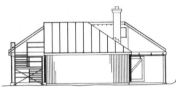

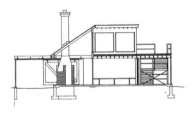

top: Pipe structure designed
and built by Yale students
in front of the Yale School of
Drama, ca. 1970.

bottom: Elevation and
section of the Arts and
Crafts Building at Camp
Cedarcrest, Orange,
Connecticut, 1968.

employed it in the "Myth Today" essay in his 1957 book, *Mythologies*: "One must naturally understand *political* in its deeper meaning," Barthes wrote, "as describing the whole of human relations in their real, social structure, in their power of making the world."[115] For Barthes, the political is active and transitive, as opposed to the "plenary, intransitive, gestural [and] theatrical" forms of depoliticized language characteristic of media-saturated late-capitalist society.[116]

The 1967 first-year building project transformed the lives of those involved, and was thus political. While not finding structural solutions to the problem of poverty in Appalachia, the process brought two disparate groups together—Ivy League students and Kentucky families—in a joint effort that resulted in actual, concrete ameliorations: a place for children to play; a roofed enclosure with toilets, a shower, and a room large enough for community dinners; a visually identifiable focus for the community. For the Kentucky families, it was important that something was actually accomplished after years of talk.

As the Yale students recounted, the process transformed them, giving them a sense of identity as full-fledged architects. Moore transformed architectural education at Yale, finding constructive focus within the establishment for his own anti-establishment impulses.[117] Finally, the program went on to transform the teaching of architecture in America by serving as a precedent for several other educational programs in which students actually build their designs.[118] Moore's achievement may best be seen as deriving from the inclusiveness and pluralism he fostered, similar to his ability as a designer to assemble multiple spatial experiences and cultural references.

In the fortuitous sequence of events that led to the first building project, Yale itself played an important role by furnishing Moore with what he needed for his innovations: a mandate for change from the school's previous leadership; a group of socially minded and enterprising students; and a commitment to a humanistic definition of the university, with its foundational belief in the transformative power of education. In this regard, it is fitting that the last words should be those of Robert A.M. Stern, the present dean of the Yale School of Architecture, who in 1986 wrote that Moore "transformed a profession by reintroducing the reality of architectural experience into the ideality of the Academy."[119]

Endnotes

1 Charles W. Moore, "You Have to Pay for the Public Life" in *Perspecta* 9–10, (New Haven: Yale School of Architecture, 1965), p. 95.

2 Kevin P. Keim, *An Architectural Life: Memoirs and Memorials of Charles W. Moore* (Boston: Little, Brown and Company, 1966), p. 127.

3 In "Charles Moore: The Architect Running in Place," Robert A.M. Stern wrote, "Moore inspired a generation of architects, a generation to which I belong, to practice architecture as an inclusive art." Eugene Johnson, ed. *Charles Moore Buildings and Projects 1949-1986* (New York: Rizzoli, 1986), p.35. In her doctoral dissertation, *Place, Time, and the Art of Architecture: The Education of Charles W. Moore* (New York University Institute of Fine Arts, 2001), Leslie L. Luebbers argues that "Moore's most profound impact on American architecture may be within the area of his activity that is most difficult to assess – education. Teaching was his calling and he went to Princeton with the express intent of becoming a leader in architectural education."

4 Martin Filler, "Charles Moore's Humane Vision" in *House Beautiful,* November 1994, Vol. 136, No. 11, p. 53.

5 See Sarah Williams Goldhagen, *Louis Kahn's Situated Modernism* (New Haven: Yale University Press, 2001), p. 126.

6 Moore was the third graduate of the doctoral program at Princeton. See Luebbers, op. cit., p. 176.

7 *Bulletin of Yale University School of Art and Architecture*, Series 62, No. 5, March 1966 (New Haven: Yale University), p. 14.

8 Robert A.M. Stern, "Yale 1950–1965" in *Oppositions* 4, October 1974, p. 36.

9 Robert A.M. Stern, in conversation with the author, January 2006.

10 Vincent Scully, *American Architecture and Urbanism* (New York: Henry Holt and Company, 1988), p. 102.

11 In "Schindler and Richardson," Moore wrote, "Bona fide vulnerability, as I see it, involves caring about the specific things you find, and find out about, so much that you will change your position to accommodate them." *Dimensions: Space, Shape, and Scale in Architecture* (New York: Architectural Record Books, 1976), pp. 168-169.

12 Robert A.M. Stern, *New Directions in American Architecture* (New York: George Braziller, 1969), p. 78.

13 [No author] "Out of the Atelier and Into Reality" in *Progressive Architecture*, September 1967, Vol. 48, p. 166.

14 Ray Gindroz letter to the author, February 2006.

15 Kent Bloomer in conversation with the author, September 2006.

16 F. Andrus Burr, "Learning Under Moore" in *GA Houses: Charles Moore and Company*, No. 7, 1980, p. 173.

17 *Bulletin of Yale University School of Art and Architecture*, Series 63, No. 1, January 1967, p. 19.

18 *Bulletin of Yale University School of Art and Architecture*, Series 61, No. 3, March 1965, p. 19.

19 Eve Blau, "Architecture or Revolution" (New Haven: Yale School of Architecture, 2000).

20 Kent Bloomer in conversation with the author, March 2005.

21 In conversations with the author, Sellers and Gluck mentioned the interest that faculty member Peter Millard took in their work.

22 In a letter to the author, M.J. Long recalled the experience: "I cut classes most Thursdays and went to Poughkeepsie to bang in nails and pour concrete. It was great and, in those days, probably the only way for a girl to get on-site building experience."

23 [No Author], "Light and Air Houses" in *Progressive Architecture*, July 1967, Vol. XLVIII, No. 7, pp. 106-115.

24 Denise Scott Brown in conversation with the author, June 2005.

25 [No Author], "Logical Land Use: Housing in Vermont that Preserves the Land" in *Architectural Forum*, December 1969, Vol. 131, No. 5, pp. 40-43.

26 C. Ray Smith, "Architecture Swings Like a Pendulum Do" in *Progressive Architecture*, May 1966, Vol. XLVII, p. 153.

27 Ibid.

28 Mary Jean Kempner, "Young Architects in the Spotlight" in *House Beautiful*, July 1966, Vol. 108, p. 69.

29 Moore once stated, "Felix [Drury] had masterminded my own Ph.D." in David Littlejohn, *Architect: The Life and Work of Charles W. Moore* (New York: Holt, Rinehart and Winston, 1984), p. 152. Drury taught at the Carnegie Institute of Technology following his graduation from Princeton, and introduced Moore to Bloomer.

30 "Out of the Atelier and Into Reality," op. cit. A year earlier, Felix Drury taught a course to second-year architecture students at the Carnegie Institute of Technology in which they designed and constructed a six-bed cabin.

31 Glenn Gregg, letter to the author, January 2006.

32 Ibid.

33 Keim, op. cit., p. 122.

34 Charles W. Moore, "The Project at New Zion: Interaction and Building" in *Eye: Magazine of the Yale Arts Association*, No. 2 (New Haven: Yale University, 1968), p. 19.

35 Charles W. Moore, "Departmental Report" in *Eye: Magazine of the Yale Arts Association*, No. 1 (New Haven: Yale University, 1967), p. 29.

36 In *Supermannerism* (New York: E.P. Dutton, 1977), p. 3, C. Ray Smith describes how "endlessly, ubiquitously repeated throughout the 1960s the words "revolution," "relevance," and "involvement" became overworked to the point of cliché. ... Everyone was "involved" with "relevant" causes. This was not mere verbiage. Real, radical activism pervaded society, and it challenged established standards, fixed principles, entrenched institutions, rigid hierarchies, and all authority."

37 Tom Carey in conversation with the author, April 2005.

38 Quoted in Keim, op. cit., pp. 123–124.

39 Tom Carey in conversation with the author, April, 2005.

40 Paul Thompson, letter to the author, August 2006.

41 Robert Swenson, letter to the author, September 2006.

42 John Morton Blum, *Years of Discord: American Politics and Society 1961–1974* (New York: W.W. Norton & Co.), p. 180.

43 David S. Walls and John B. Stephenson, *Appalachia in the Sixties: A Decade of Reawakening* (Lexington: The University Press of Kentucky, 1972), pp. xiii-xiv.

44 Harry M. Caudill, *The Watches of the Night* (Boston: Little, Brown and Company, 1976), pp. 21–22.

45 Robert Coles and Joseph Brenner, "American Youth in a Social Struggle: The Appalachian Volunteers" in *American Journal of Orthopsychiatry*, Vol. 38, 1968, p. 31.

46 Burr, op. cit.

47 Alberto Lau, "A Meeting of Needs" in *Yale Alumni Magazine*, October 1967, Vol. XXXI, No. 1, p. 36.

48 Tom Carey in conversation with the author, November 2005.

49 Moore, "The Project at New Zion," op. cit.

50 Robert Swenson, letter to the author, September 2006.

51 Alberto Lau, "New Zion Community Center: A New Experience in Architectural Education" in *Progressive Architecture*, September 1967, Vol. 48, p. 167.

52 Lau, "A Meeting of Needs," op. cit.

53 Moore, "The Project at New Zion," op. cit.

54 Lau, "New Zion Community Center: A New Experience in Architectural Education," op. cit.

55 Moore, "The Project at New Zion," op. cit.

56 Burr, op. cit.

57 Sea Ranch was featured on the cover of the May 1966 issue of *Progressive Architecture*, for example.

58 Burr, op. cit. Daniel V. Scully described the Center in New Zion as a "Sea Ranch-derivative scheme" in conversation with the author, April 2005.

59 Lau, "New Zion Community Center: New Experience in Architectural Education" op. cit., p. 168.

60 James Volney Righter, letter to the author, July 2006.

61 Lau, op cit., p. 169.

62 Ibid.

63 Ibid.

64 Ibid.

65 Ibid.

66 Daniel V. Scully in conversation with the author, April 2005.

67 Lau, op. cit.

68 Moore, "The Project at New Zion," op. cit.

69 Lau, op. cit.

70 Ibid.

71 Ibid.

72 Burr, op. cit., p. 174.

73 Stern, "Charles Moore: The Architect Running in Place," op. cit., p. 36.

74 Denise Scott Brown, "Learning the Wrong Lessons from the Beaux-Arts" in *AD Profiles 17: The Beaux-Arts* (London, 1979), p. 32.

75 Mark Ellis, "Yale Goes to Kentucky: An Account of the Lower Grassy-Trace Branch Community Center Project" in *Interiors*, December 1968, Vol. CXXXVII, p. 137.

76 As in the previous year, graduates of Williams and Yale Colleges predominated in the winning team. Douglas and Hager attended Yale, while Ellis and Shepler attended Williams. Leopold is a Radcliffe alumna.

77 Ellis, op. cit., p. 138.

78 Ibid., p. 139.

79 Ibid., p. 140.

80 Ellen Leopold letter to the author, February 2006.

81 Moore, "The Project at New Zion," op. cit., p. 18.

82 Scott Brown, op. cit. Richard Chafee, however, has noted that the term *patron*, in contradistinction to *maitre*, struck a note of familiarity and connoted a bond of friendship. In "The Teaching of Architecture at the École des Beaux-Arts" in *The Architecture of the École des Beaux-Arts*, ed. Arthur Drexler (New York: The Museum of Modern Art, 1977), p. 95.

83 Donald Drew Egbert, *The Beaux-Arts Tradition in French Architecture* (Princeton: Princeton University Press, 1980), p. 147.

84 Richard Ellmann, *Oscar Wilde* (New York: Vintage Books, 1988), pp. 49-50.

85 R. Buckminster Fuller, "The Cardboard House" in *Perspecta* Vol. 2, 1953 (New Haven: Yale School of Architecture, 1953), pp. 28-30.

86 Scully, Louis I. Kahn, op. cit., p. 21.

87 Vincent Scully, *American Architecture and Urbanism* (New York: Henry Holt and Company, 1988), p. 8.

88 Christian Bjone, *First House* (Chichester, West Sussex: John Wiley & Sons, 2002), pp. 202-211.

89 In "The Project at New Zion," op cit., p. 18, Moore stated that the building project "has been extensively and well-described in the technical and general press."

90 C. Ray Smith, "The New Interiors: Fact or Fad?" in *Progressive Architecture*, October 1968, Vol. XLIX, p. 150.

91 Littlejohn, op. cit., p. 12.

92 C. Ray Smith, *Supermannerism*, op. cit., p. xxvii. Ada Louise Huxtable, in "Kicked a Building Lately?", described Yale as one of the "more 'with-it' architectural schools." (*The New York Times*, January 12, 1969, p. 25).

93 Burr, op. cit., p. 175, described how Sellers "became widely known for his Prickly Mountain houses, some of which appeared in the first "Forty Under Forty" exhibit. Sellers built them while still a student and his direct, Vermont chain-saw approach to architecture was admired by his contemporaries."

94 [No Author], "Putney Students Build a Dorm," in *Progressive Architecture*, May 1967, Vol. XLVIII, pp. 102-6.

95 Jean Progner, "Student Housing Comes Alive" in *Progressive Architecture*, September 1968, Vol. XLIV, p. 24. In a letter to the author in April 2006, Edward D'Andrea wrote, "David Sellers was the wavy gravy and Ringo Reinecke was the best damn framer I ever met."

96 Smith, *Supermannerism*, op. cit.

97 Smith, "The New Interiors: Fact or Fad?" op cit., p. 154.

98 For 1968, see Arthur Marwick, *The Sixties: Cultural Revolution in Britain, France, Italy and the United States, c. 1958–1974* (Oxford: Oxford University Press, 1998), pp. 584-678.

99 Blau, op. cit.

100 Smith, "The New Interior: Fact or Fad?" op. cit., p. 152.

101 Huxtable, op. cit., p. 25.

102 For Stauffacher's work at Sea Ranch, see [No Author], "Bathhouse Graphics: Make it Happy, Kid" in *Progressive Architecture*, March 1967, Vol. XLVIII, pp. 156-161.

103 Smith: "The New Interior: Fact or Fad?" op. cit.

104 Huxtable, op. cit., p. 25.

105 For the Columbia riots, see Marwick, op cit, pp. 656–665. See also the editorial in the June 20, 1968 issue of *The New York Times*, "Harnessing the Youth Tide."

106 Ellis, op. cit., p. 136.

107 [No author], "Yale Men Build Fresh Air Camp" in *The New York Times*, July 5, 1968, p. 23. In a letter to the author, Ellen Leopold noted that three of these "Yale Men" were women—Mazie Cox, Susan St. John, and herself.

108 William Borders, "Yale Students Mold an Experimental House of Plastic Foam" in *The New York Times*, June 18, 1968.

109 Clinton A. Page, "Foam House" in *Progressive Architecture*, May, 1971, Vol. 52, pp. 100–103.

110 Daniel V. Scully in conversation with the author, December 2005.

111 Robert Brustein in conversation with the author, September 2005.

112 Robert Brustein, *Making Scenes: A Personal History of the Turbulent Years at Yale 1966–1979* (New York: Random House, 1981), p. 70.

113 For the projects by Robert Venturi, see David B. Brownlee, et al., *Out of the Ordinary: Robert Venturi, Denise Scott Brown and Associates* (Philadelphia: Philadelphia Museum of Art, 2001), pp. 16-28. Michael Curtis does not remember having seen illustrations of Venturi's beach house project.

114 Letter from Roc Caivano to the author, February 2005.

115 Roland Barthes, *Mythologies*, trans., Annette Lavers (New York: Farrar, Strauss & Giroux, 1972), p. 143.

116 Ibid., p. 144.

117 Charles Moore, "The Establishment invites you to join in hushed and sumptuous appreciation of the several arts ..." in *Architectural Forum*, September 1966, Vol. 125, pp. 71-79.

118 In 1970, David Sellers set up an architectural program at Goddard College in northern Vermont, in which hands-on building was an important feature, that lasted for six years. Today, he continues his work with design-build at the Vermont school, Yestermorrow, founded in 1980 by Yale alumnus John Connell. From 2002–2006 Bruce Lindsey, an alumnus of the Yale School of Architecture, served as co-director of the "Rural Studio" at Auburn University. One of Lindsey's first-year Yale class-mates, Bryan Bell, carries forward the social imper-atives of the First-Year Building Project through his organization Design Corps. William Sherman, a member of the class of 1982, helped initiate a program in the Department of Architecture and Landscape Architecture at the University of Virginia based on Yale's model. Louise Harpman of the class of 1993 established DESIGN> BUILD>TEXAS at the University of Texas after teaching at Yale for seven years.

119 Stern, "Charles Moore: The Architect Running in Place," op. cit., p. 37.

Thirty-Five Years of Teaching Yale Students to Build:
Interview with Paul B. Brouard

Richard Hayes: Paul, you have taught at Yale for thirty-five years now. During that time, the Building Project has been a remarkable success. Why, and how, did you start to teach at Yale; what have been your educational goals; and how has the program changed under your stewardship?

Paul Brouard: I started studying here at Yale in 1957, one year prior to Paul Rudolph's chairmanship, and then three years while he led the school. It was a four-year program at that time and we received a bachelor of architecture degree. Five years after I graduated, Yale sent me a letter that said, "If you send us thirty-five dollars, we'll send you a master's degree." It's one of the best bargains I ever got! They had changed the program into a master's program.

RH: Was Rudolph interested in having students build while they were still in school?

PB: Not as an academic effort. I know that a lot of students worked for him, but the kind of work that he was doing was not hands-on while I was at school. I worked for some of the other architects who were teaching here, such as Charlie Brewer, and for them, we did hands-on work. There was no intention to educate for building.

RH: Did you have a background in building before coming to Yale?

PB: Yes, I came from a building tradition. I had already designed and built a few houses, and I had designed and supervised the construction of large jamboree camps for the Girl Scouts throughout the country. So I came to Yale with a considerable amount of practical experience, and I was appalled by the fact that there was nothing in the curriculum that addressed the idea of architecture as a built art. Frankly, I never got over that!

RH: What about your classmates?

PB: I will say that the people I went to school with suffered from the fact that there was no building art involved with what they were doing. I stayed in close contact with a number of classmates, who later had difficulty adjusting to some of the rigors of the profession which require you to be out in the field and work with contractors. After graduating from Yale, I worked as an architect for fifteen years. First, I worked three years for John Johansen, who had a practice in New Canaan. While I was there, we designed a number of theaters, such as the Morris Mechanic Theater in Baltimore, the Mummers Theater in Kansas City, and a project for an experimental theater for Vassar that was never built. I also did construction supervision on the library at Clark University, in Worcester, Massachusetts, which was built just after Rudolph's Art & Architecture Building was finished.

RH: While you were practicing, Charles W. Moore started to teach at Yale.

PB: Yes. Charlie Moore had been here for a few years and had established the Building Project, and they had completed four projects before I came aboard. I heard about the Building Project through a friend of Kent Bloomer's and in 1971 I contacted Kent and said that I was very interested in the idea. Kent volunteered me to work with them on a sun and shade shelter on the beach in Guilford, Connecticut, which was my first building project. The school then took me on to work in the field with the students. I loved working outdoors, and I loved to build. So, for eighteen years before we started building the individual houses, I worked from about the first of April until the first of July, which was the time frame in which the students detailed their projects and then went out and built them. In the early years, for the most part, I was finished by July.

RH: Has that changed in terms of the time frame and goals of the project?

top: Photograph of Paul B. Brouard, 2003.
middle: Photograph of Beach Pavilion in Guilford, Connecticut, 1971.
bottom: Photograph of Cabin Creek Medical Center, Dawes, West Virginia, 1975.

PB: When we started building the houses in 1989, the whole process changed. The time involved, the amount of detailing needed, and the building time required—it all steam-rolled to the point where it is now a year-round commitment. From May first until the time the building is finished I spend about a thousand hours working in the field, and during the rest of the year I do the prep work for the following year's project. The role we play with contributors, such as keeping in contact with them and submitting grant proposals is a large part of the program.

RH: Let's go back to the first project you worked on, the 1971 pavilion in Guilford. Was the system in place so that you could come in and lead the field part of it, or was the organization of the overall Project still developing?

PB: There was really no system when I started. There were the students who were really interested and were putting time into the project, and then there were the students who were not so interested. Nevertheless, everybody would get out there.

RH: What caused the change in program from community centers in rural Appalachia to the series of beach pavilions and park buildings in New England—the projects built in the later seventies and early eighties?

PB: Each project depended upon individual circumstances. For example, in 1975 I led a project in West Virginia that had originated in a suggestion made by a student, Jonathan Kammel. It was a medical center in a region called Cabin Creek. When Kammel introduced that project to us, along with the $75,000 grant that the client had in place, we said, "Let's do it!"

RH: It does seem that student initiative has been an important part of the Building Project from the very beginning of the program. To a large extent, students founded the first project, the community center in New Zion, Kentucky. Denise Scott Brown remarked to me that Yale architecture students were more enterprising and entrepreneurial than other students she taught in the late sixties and early seventies.

PB: The history of the program is reflected in the changing of the building types. There are many reasons why we do not do certain things anymore. For example, when I took the class to West Virginia, I was responsible for that whole class for two or three months. There really wasn't any problem until we were building the roof, and some men drove by and fired a couple of shots toward us. I could tell you a couple of stories about New Haven like that, too!

RH: Were there any other reasons why that was the last project in Appalachia?

PB: I think that the cost of moving people out of state became prohibitive, and I also think that the expectations of the students changed and some were unable to leave their personal and professional commitments. We were in West Virginia for three months, living in a dormitory at Morris Harvey College (which was an experience in itself). The college was a fifteen-mile commute to the site where we worked at Cabin Creek. Arrangements had been made to feed us at the college. The food proved to be quite heavy, so we negotiated a stipend to do our own cooking. The sponsors of the project prepared our midday meal, which gave us the opportunity to socialize and get to know these special people. But, since then, the projects have been local. Herb Newman, project coordinator, became more involved and started negotiating for projects. His contacts in New Haven and also in some of the neighboring towns were invaluable. The projects that were park shelters, beach pavilions, and concert stages were generated out of Herb's contacts. It was through Herb that we did the camp buildings near New Haven, such as Camp Farnam in Durham and Camp Laurelwood in Madison. For four summers, we designed and built camp buildings. They were great, because they were all on lakes. We were there in May and June when the camp was not in operation, so we could use some of the camp facilities. When we designed the dormitory and conference center for the Boy Scout

top: Photograph of Cohen Memorial Lodge, Camp Sequassen, Winsted, Connecticut, 1980.
bottom: Photograph of Paul Brouard and students with model of the 1989 house for Habitat for Humanity of Greater New Haven.

camp in Winsted, Connecticut, we lived in the cabins and prepared our own meals, which we ate in the dining halls. The owners gave us the keys to their food lockers and the phone numbers of their local food purveyors. One of the students, Daniel Brown, had been a pastry chef, and he was ecstatic when we found a freezer that was filled with surplus butter. He used to get up at four o'clock in the morning to bake all kinds of great delicacies for us!

RH: After these pavilions and camp buildings, why was there a shift to the individual houses—first for Habitat for Humanity, then for Neighborhood Housing Services (NHS)?

PB: I think it was of the time. We felt that we had been doing community service, but that we could do something even more significant by working with the housing stock in New Haven. A graduate of the school, Kari Nordstrom, who now works as an architect for the Office of Facility Management at Yale, approached us with the idea. He was on the board of Habitat for Humanity, and he asked me if we would be interested in building houses. Our collaboration with Habitat caused a dramatic change in many of the expectations for the whole program. The idea of having to complete a building that was not just a structure, but also had all of the mechanical and other amenities that you need in a residential building, is fantastically comprehensive for the students. As learning experiences, the pavilions were great structural and expressive exercises. But I think that it's much more challenging to start your education by designing and constructing a building that has a full program and also has the personal aspect of being a house built for a real family in a local neighborhood.

RH: Would you say that there is one project that stands out in terms of the educational value for the students?

PB: In general, I think that every one of the houses has been a learning experience that meets the goal of our program. When we started with Habitat, we were not required to do all of the finishing, which was done by their volunteers. Their philosophy was that they wanted to get as much housing for every dollar they spent as quickly as possible. They were not interested in spending extra time or money in detailing and crafting buildings. I had some contacts with the people at NHS, which has a local chapter in New Haven, and I showed their construction superintendent our projects. They had built new row houses, but there was such a need for rehabilitating existing buildings that they only worked on restorations and renovations at the time. We began to work with them in 1996 and did the only new construction in their annual production of over thirty residential units.

RH: Was there also a project for an organization called Home, Inc.?

PB: Yes, we did two houses for Habitat and then, in 1991, we did a house on Blake Street in New Haven for Home, Inc. That was a two-family rental house that became part of a further development on the same site when Home, Inc. put up another six units that were all prefabricated. Home, Inc. is a non-profit organization that builds or renovates buildings to rent, not sell. We were more interested in building for homeowners rather than renters, so we built four more houses for Habitat. Since 1996, we have finished eleven houses for NHS; they operate on a business-like basis and improved the efficiency of our program. More importantly, our students have had real opportunities for custom designing and for exploring craftsmanship. I think it has been evident that NHS supports us designing unique buildings with significant, crafted parts. The first few houses were very straightforward. We were able to include some crafted aspects in the design of the porches and in some of the cabinetwork. Staircases also had crafted elements. In the last few years, this has expanded. One very interesting project was the 2004 house, in which a combined stair-and-bookcase element was designed on the computer, and the component pieces were all cut using CNC (Computer Numerically Controlled) technology. The machine cut highly intricate

Photograph of bookcase
and stair in the 2004 house
for Neighborhood Housing
Services of New Haven.

shapes out of plywood—it was amazing! Thirty-nine sheets of plywood were used to make over 400 individual pieces fit together—it was a very complex structure. An alumnus, Louis Mackall, who has a modern woodworking shop in Guilford called Breakfast Woodworks, donated the use of his machine. Five students worked eleven weeks to design, cut, and assemble this sculptural element for the house.

RH: Have the computer technologies enhanced the projects?

PB: The CNC process does allow the students to apply new technologies and learn new skills. We have also talked about doing more prefabrication of building parts, not just of detail parts. However, I feel very strongly that the stick-built building is a very good way to learn. Understanding how prefabrication works, and how you manage it and design with it takes years of experience to do well.

RH: Besides your work with suppliers and donors, you have also incorporated environmental and green building elements in the recent projects. How did this come about, and will it be a standardized aspect of the Project from now on?

PB: For the past decade, we have experimented with technologies and materials, some of which have been very successful and which we are still using. A student initiative ten years ago got us started on some of the environmental issues. One student, Jeff Goldstein, put us in touch with a company that makes foam building insulation; they have been donating the material, which is very expensive, ever since. Our buildings have received a high Energy Star rating for the past six years. We have incorporated mechanical systems such as "air recovery," which takes fresh air and mixes it with the air in the building and heats it with the air going out. Another manufacturer donated that equipment, and we put it in the 2000 house on West Read Street. One of the problems we face, however, when we put in experimental systems or components, is that many of the households are first-time homeowners who need education in using and caring for these systems. So, NHS has set up a Homeowner's Center, which is an educational facility for their homeowners, and they conduct regular classes. New homeowners are required to attend the classes.

RH: What other environmental systems and technologies have you incorporated in the houses?

PB: When mechanical engineer Ev Barber was teaching at Yale, he donated a solar system for hot water to the 1994 house built with Habitat for Humanity. The 2005 project received an educational grant of $25,000 from the Clean Energy Fund of Connecticut to install an electric solar system. The system uses solar energy to provide more than fifty percent of the electricity for the building. There was a lot of interest by the state, and the mayor of New Haven came to the site to meet the installer of the system. An alumnus, Lindsay Suter, who has a practice in Branford, was instrumental in helping us to apply for the grant. A student, Gabrielle Brainard, followed through on the application. When we realized that we would have a $5,000 shortfall in terms of installing the system, we went back to the state and—partly because of the fact that this was a student project for affordable housing—it contributed the additional $5,000.

RH: How much of a role do the students have in determining the design of the house?

PB: The students' role in the team format is to design the house. We provide the consultancy to guide the decisions so that the submissions are competitive in the design and engineered for construction. The design faculty works first with individual house designs by each student, and then with the ten student teams in preparation for the jury that chooses the building to be built. The consultants are responsible for providing students with expertise needed for construction. As preparation for the beginning of the design phase, building, neighborhood, and urban issues, as well as structural and

top: Photograph of the 1986
Education Pavilion at Fort
Nathan Hale.
bottom: Photograph of
the 1987 band shell in
Bridgeport, Connecticut.

mechanical codes, material, and construction practices, are presented in the classroom. The consulting team is composed of faculty, outside professional specialists, building officials, and construction experts. Each student team has a teaching assistant to advise and guide the process. Individual class members are elected to an administrative body that organizes the work, such as scheduling, presentation, budgets, and contributions. Making the process work involves fifty students, ten faculty members, six teaching assistants, fifteen consultants, eight city officials, forty donors, four developer representatives—all enthusiastic about learning and doing.

The final team design is the result of this collaboration. When a design is selected to be built, the entire class joins the process to red line the design, making revisions that transform the team design so that it is taken to the field for construction by all.

RH: How does the budget for the house enter the design process? At what point does understanding what their design is going to cost and whether it can be realistically achieved enter the picture for the first-year students?

PB: As part of the studio process, each team presents the budget for its building in a fairly strict format. I give them basic information about costs on a quantity basis, adjusted for the labor and material donation. Each team's calculation is part of the presentation when we select a building. We use that document from the winning scheme to judge where we are—in terms of what goes on in the field, and the cost of various building elements. We monitor the cost as we move forward. But if something comes up that is not within the scope of the budget, then the students have to see whether they can get it as a donation, or they have to choose another material or find another way of building it. It is amazing that they can actually produce a good design, and then do working drawings, all in five weeks. Any architect's office would take several months, but a lot of the student success is the team effort and collaborative process.

RH: How long have the students been doing complete sets of working drawings?

PB: On the early projects, I went out in the field with what were essentially cartoons; we solved how the building really went together in the field. Doing full sets of drawings has been going on now only for the last five or six years. Even for the first few houses, we built from rough drawings. It was more like design-build then, as the projects were detailed in the field. Now we are going out with quite sophisticated drawings, but they still get revised and reworked, and sometimes completely overridden in the field.

RH: Do Yale students today have much building experience before coming to school?

PB: Many of the students today have experience with office work. In the 1970s, students started to go out and build, but it did not last for a very long time. By 1980, not too many people were going out and building. Alan Organschi, who coordinates the Building Project studio, does have a design-build practice today. He worked on the 1986 project—the education pavilion in Fort Nathan Hale Park—that was a very sophisticated design in prefabricated concrete and steel. More recently, there have been people like Ben Bischoff, Oliver Freundlich, and Brian Papa with their New York firm called MADE. But when I hear back from a lot of the students, it seems that there are very few who are doing very much hands-on building.

RH: What about the Charles Moore continuum, such as Centerbrook architects Mark Simon, Jefferson Riley, and Chad Floyd—how were they influenced by the Building Project?

PB: I worked with Chad Floyd on that first Guilford project. There's no question that they are committed to the idea of good building. One student, Darin Cook, went on to work for them. At Yale, he ran the concert pavilion project in 1987 in Bridgeport, which took two years to complete. Darin was shameless about asking for contributions—like going to Citytrust Bank and asking for a $50,000 donation for the copper for the roof! This effort instigated asking for outside support for our projects.

RH: How would you describe the educational goal of the Building Project?

PB: It is an academic project to teach an understanding about building, and to be able to work with the client, consultants, and the building industry. I am not training people to go out and become builders. But I do want them to construct a complete building. I want the students to go into the ground with a foundation and I want them to stick build pieces that make a structure and finish a project. I see this as an opportunity for the students to understand the building process with their own physical labor. It is something they absolutely need. You cannot be a good architect without understanding building, and being able to deal knowledgeably with the people who are constructing your building.

RH: How do you see the Building Project moving forward?

PB: The longevity and development of our work has been gratifying. For nine years I have been working with Adam Hopfner, who is now well versed in the administration of the Project, and we are in the process of transitioning our roles in the studio and the field with the strong support of Dean Stern. The goals of the Project will meet the challenge of technology advancement, while still recognizing the value of hands-on learning.

From Appalachia to New Haven:
The First-Year Building Project Since 1975

As the First-Year Building Project emerged from the crucible of the nine-teen-sixties, it remained true to its original commitment to experiential education and community service, evolving as needed, yet continuing with notable fidelity the process established in 1967 as if self-propelled, despite changes in architectural culture. Certainly, one of the principal reasons for its longevity, continuity, and success has been the contribution of Paul B. Brouard, a member of the class of 1961 who joined the faculty in 1971 and has led the construction phase of the program ever since. Brouard's commit-ment to the Building Project has been limitless, and his remarkable com-bination of building knowledge, educational skills, good humor, and spirit of fun has been a guiding light for Yale students for almost thirty-six years. Indeed, many graduates of the school attest that the First-Year Building Project was the most memorable, enjoyable, and valuable part of their archi-tectural education at Yale.

Inevitably, there have been bumps along the way. The community centers built in 1967, 1968, and 1969 were all demolished, as were the 1969 play device at Camp Cedarcrest and the 1971 beach structures in Guilford, Connecticut. The 1969 community center for the Long River Village pub-lic housing project in Middletown may be seen as a paradigmatic story of idealism confronting the hard facts of reality, not negotiable by architecture alone. The ambitious, 4,000-square-foot, masonry and steel building took almost two years to build and represented the best of intentions on the part of the students and community organizers. Yet, funding for actual programs at the center was never secured, and, following changes in leadership at the Middletown Housing Authority, the vacant building was declared structurally unsound and torn down. It may serve as a cautionary tale in the vicissitudes of students' trying their hands at the time-consuming process of masonry construction or entering into the thicket of entrenched municipal politics, but the recollections of some of the students involved have a rueful note. That shared quality suggests the relevance of poet William Blake's tripartite model of youthful idealism followed by experience, leading to a chastened innocence—true for many who came of age during the nineteen-sixties.[1]

Moore's opening up of the graduate curriculum, of which the 1967 build-ing project was the fullest expression, may have had unintentional, even wayward, side effects while he was still teaching at Yale. During their second year, for example, members of the class of 1972 set up a studio on George Street as an alternative to the School of Architecture, in order to pursue extracurricular design-build projects. Working in what they described as a spirit of democratic collaboration, they eventually designed and built houses in Colorado, Vermont, and New Mexico.[2] In the December 1970 issue of *SENSUS*, a magazine published by the Schools of Art and Architecture, the students' enthusiasm for their initiative included rather bold criticism of their teachers: "The faculty are not sufficiently committed to the designing of the curriculum nor perceptive enough of the educational needs of stu-dents."[3] Gerald Allen, one of the editors of *SENSUS*, took note of the School's "'loose' curriculum which has in a sense been one spur to their own experi-ment and which also comes under their strong criticism."[4] Like Yale presi-dent Kingman Brewster, Jr. during these years, Moore often took the heat for the latitude he extended to students.[5]

Unquestionably, the School of Architecture went through a difficult period following on events in 1969 that included the suspension of classes, the dismantling of the City Planning Department, and a three-alarm fire in the Art & Architecture Building.[6] The student activism that contributed to the formation of the First-Year Building Project also found expression in pro-test marches, demonstrations, and guerrilla theater events that may have

top: Photograph of the
Long River Village
Community Center in
Middletown, Connecticut,
ca. 1970.
middle: Photograph of
200 York Street in
New Haven, Connecticut,
renovated by the
Student Community
Housing Corporation,
ca. 1971.
bottom: Photograph of
Cabin Creek Medical
Center, Dawes, West
Virginia.

attracted interest away from the study of architecture.[7] A generously granted Out-of-Residence Program added to the open atmosphere. Members of the class of 1972 Brink Thorne and Richard Shepard, for example, submitted an application to this program to study what they called "psychological anticipatory spaces." They proceeded to buy a Land Rover in London and drove around the world for thirteen months.[8]

Other activities reflected Moore's belief in social progress. Moore forged a connection to Black America by inviting activist Colin ("Topper") Carew to give a series of lectures, and, with Moore's support, a group of ten students founded the Black Workshop in 1968 as a community-oriented student-activist group working out of a storefront on Chapel Street. The group provided advocacy services intended to help revitalize New Haven's African-American neighborhoods, particularly The Hill, and eventually became the Black Environmental Studies Team (B.E.S.T.), the first director of which was Richard K. Dozier of the class of 1970.[9]

In 1969, another group of students and faculty formed a non-profit, tax-exempt organization called the Student Community Housing Corporation, under the aegis of which they purchased an apartment building on York Street in New Haven and renovated it as low- and moderate-income housing for students and the elderly.[10] Based on the thesis project of Robert Knight of the class of 1970, the renovation was supported by HUD, and Moore donated his time as consulting architect.[11] The renovation anticipated the concentration on affordable housing in New Haven that would occur in the Building Project twenty years later.

One of the last building projects to take place while Moore was still on the faculty was one of the most ambitious and most successful expressions of the program's activist origins. In 1975, students designed the Cabin Creek Medical Center, a 7,500-square-foot medical facility in Dawes, West Virginia, a hamlet in a poverty-stricken region with a long history of coal mining. Members of the class of 1977 moved to West Virginia, living for five weeks during the spring of 1975 at a local college while they built the clinic, which had been founded to alleviate black lung disease among miners. The fourth and last project by Yale students in Appalachia, the Cabin Creek Medical Center continues to serve its community, and is today prominently featured on the clinic's website.

"A simple building:" Pavilions and Recreation Structures of the 1970s and 1980s

The shift to more modest projects during the nineteen-seventies and eighties may be seen as an internal correction that followed a few overly ambitious projects that took years to complete and seemed to meet their demise soon thereafter. It also reflects the tightened economy of the mid-seventies. During the period 1973 to 1988, students completed over sixteen projects, ranging from wood-framed cabins at a camp for underprivileged children in Durham, Connecticut, to a copper-sheathed band shell in down-town Bridgeport. Herbert S. Newman, a member of the class of 1959, who served as a design critic since the first building project, took the lead in finding clients for these projects, many of which developed out of his own professional contacts as a prominent architect in New Haven. Appointed project coordinator in 1973, Newman had cogent reasons for giving the recreational structures and pavilions as design problems, since they allowed the students to focus on basic architectural facts, such as site and solar orientation, the creation of place, and elemental structural forces.[12] In a concise article entitled "First-Year Building Project: Learning Experience and Community Service," published in the Winter 1980 issue of the *Journal of Architecture Education*, Newman summarized his and his colleagues' objectives:

> *A simple building with a single program forces the student to deal on an intimate level with the question of how to build. This process brings the*

top: Photograph of meeting-
house, Village of Niantic,
Connecticut.
bottom: Drawing from
the frontispiece of *Essai
sur l'architecture* by
Marc-Antoine Laugier,
1755 edition.

*student architect perhaps closer than he or she will ever be to the
tradition of the "master builder." How to keep it from falling down and how
to make it provide shelter are often triggers to unique, original expressions
of architecture as art.*[13]

The students enjoyed the pavilion and camp projects of the seventies and
eighties located in picturesque parts of Connecticut. Alumnus Robert Works,
for example, observed of the Hopkins Pavilion on the shore of Powers Lake
in East Lyme, built in 1981 for the Yale Outdoor Education Center: "It was
a blast. The experience of communal living at the camp, after a long year
in New Haven, was idyllic."[14] His words seem to fulfill Newman's hope for
the students that spending the spring and summer months outside of New
Haven would be "both unifying and liberating, after confinement in the
studio all winter."[15] Works's classmate, Aaron Betsky, similarly remembers
the East Lyme project as a "tremendous experience," due in large part to
the beautiful setting. "Designing and constructing something...in [such a]
romantic setting as eastern Connecticut reinforced the sense of the relationship between buildings and landscape, which teachers like Vincent Scully
and Charles Moore had made us aware of," Betsky recalls.[16] The emphasis
on the experiential value of the building projects during these years resonated with Moore's and Bloomer's argument for a direct, physical engagement with architecture in their 1977 book, *Body, Memory, and Architecture.*

Living and working in these rural settings encouraged the students' initiative, often expressed through their ingenuity in preparing communal meals.
This was especially true for the 1980 project for a dormitory and conference center at Camp Sequassen in New Hartford (formerly Winsted),
Connecticut, where Daniel Brown, now an architect in New Zealand, used his
background as a pastry chef for the benefit of his classmates. One of those
classmates, Kay Bea Jones, found the project "a grounding experience" for
her personally, with a particular value for female architectural students. Now
a professor of architecture at Ohio State University, Jones observed:

*Hands-on craft and seeing a design from concept to execution gave me a
hold on why I was interested in architecture and the confidence to perse-
vere. Paul Brouard offered opportunities to women students, who may have
been less likely to have been on job sites, getting their hands on tools and
materials. This empowered female students (who he thought were often the
most capable). Italian has a word that English does not:* grinta, *like chutz-
pah, means the drive, desire, and capacity to do tough things. Working with
Paul and my classmates on the building project, I found my* grinta.[17]

The 1980 project was also an important milestone for William Sherman, the
lead designer for the selected scheme, an elegant wood structure evocative of
Scandinavian architecture. Currently the chair of the Department of Architecture
and Landscape Architecture at the University of Virginia, Sherman has recently
overseen the start-up of a program there based on Yale's Building Project, and
he incorporates design-build strategies in his own architectural practice.

The last of the pavilion projects was a meeting hall built in the form of a barn
next to the restored nineteenth century Smith Harris House in the village of
Niantic, Connecticut, and it follows Newman's idea of the simple program
that allows student architects to be "master builders." The 1,500-square-
foot barn has a minimalist exterior of cedar siding that sheathes an interior
defined by heavy timber trusses. Roberto Espejo, a member of the class of
1990, considers the design for the timber barn as participating in a lineage
leading back to the primitive hut described by the eighteenth-century theorist, Marc-Antoine Laugier.[18] Constructing such a seemingly primitive hut
inspired the students to devise ad hoc rituals as well:

*Every Friday there was some sort of milestone event, meant to reflect on
the week's progress. The most memorable was the famous "truss-dancing"*

top: Opening day of the
1994 house on Dewitt Street.
bottom: Photograph of the
1992 house on Newhall
Street, both for Habitat
for Humanity of Greater
New Haven.

*party. Once the timber trusses had been fully fabricated, a Herculean
task, a party ignited in which students, faculty, and even the client found
themselves in a conga line, each holding pieces of honey-basted chicken,
over the narrow eight-inch width of each and every truss. Music blasted,
there was a lot of laughter, as well as pensive contemplation by smaller
groups who wanted to celebrate in a quiet way. We felt that we were
part of something larger than any of us. Later, around a campfire at the
evening's end, we realized that the class of 1990's party had become a
primal response to the beauty of building.[19]*

Affordable Housing

The celebration described by Espejo could almost be seen as the coda to
an era, for a year later, in 1989, the Building Project moved away from these
"simple buildings" to a commitment to affordable housing in New Haven
that has lasted for eighteen years. During the tenure of Thomas Beeby as
dean, Kari Nordstrom, an alumnus of the school and a board member of the
New Haven chapter of Habitat for Humanity, proposed the idea of working
with the Georgia-based non-profit to Brouard and Newman, who negotiated a contract between the organization and the university. According to
Newman, the suggestion brought into focus a perception shared by several
faculty members that it was time for the Building Project to respond to the
pressing needs of New Haven.[20] A concern for low-income housing could
be viewed as part of Moore's legacy at Yale, to the extent that such work was
an important—if as yet unstudied—component of Moore's own career as an
architect. Moore completed affordable housing projects in Orono, Maine;
Huntington, New York; and Middletown, Connecticut, in addition to the
Church Street South houses in New Haven. With Yale students Ronald Filson
and Thomas Rapp, Moore designed an award-winning scheme for federally
funded housing in Whitesburg, Kentucky, that was never built.[21]

The shift to individual houses may also reflect other currents in postmodern
architectural culture, such as the renewed interest in the typological forms
of domestic architecture by Robert Venturi, and the revival of neighborhood-
based, traditional forms of city planning by Yale-trained New Urbanists
Andres Duany and Elizabeth Plater-Zyberk, both members of the class of
1974.[22] It was during these years that Vincent Scully, always an important
influence at Yale, emphasized the theme of the architecture of community in
his lectures. In the larger culture, the popularity of *This Old House* on public
television reflected a burgeoning interest in the domestic sphere, as related
to a hands-on, do-it-yourself culture.

But for the students, what mattered was the social responsibility of building
affordable housing in some of New Haven's poorest neighborhoods. As Michael
Wetstone, a member of the class of 1991 who worked on the first residential
project—the 1989 two-family house on Hallock Street in The Hill—recalls:

*I think that the beginning of the Habitat for Humanity projects in our year
gave a revitalizing boost to the Building Project, due to the direct social
purpose and the presence of a real client who would actually live in the
house. This lent a seriousness to the endeavor, which caused personal and
aesthetic issues to recede somewhat.[23]*

For Brouard, the educational value involved in designing and building
houses for actual homeowners embodied a quantum leap forward in the
Building Project. The change in building type required a greater level of
organization, management, and stratification of the program. In contrast
to its early years, which were rather informal, the program became highly
structured, involving a cadre of teaching assistants and students elected
to perform very specific roles, in addition to intensive efforts to secure
donated materials from manufacturers and vendors. Using up-to-date computer programs, students today produce thorough, sophisticated sets of
working drawings that could be the envy of many professional offices.

top: Photograph of the 2000 house on West Read Street. middle: Photograph of 2001 house on Fifth Street. bottom: Photograph of 2003 house on Porter Street.

The recent increase in class size has also led to a tighter organization of on-site construction. These themes are explored in a handbook funded by the Graham Foundation, published in 1996 by the School of Architecture, intended to help other schools devise similar programs.[24]

After building six houses in conjunction with Habitat for Humanity and a two-family house for a New-Haven-based non-profit organization called Home, Inc., the program joined forces in 1996 with Neighborhood Housing Services of New Haven (NHS). A non-profit, community development organization that is part of the national Neighborhood Housing Services of America, NHS has made significant impact on New Haven through a program of restoring existing, often abandoned, houses. Their work in conjunction with the Yale School of Architecture is their only new construction, and they have just completed their eleventh house together with Yale, a single-family house on Henry Street in the Dixwell Avenue neighborhood. Typically 1,500 square feet in size and comprising three bedrooms, in addition to living and dining rooms, kitchen, and bathroom, the eleven houses are located throughout New Haven. All of the completed houses are occupied by first-time homeowners.

The six residences built for Habitat for Humanity tended to be traditional in design, with frontal gables, street-facing porches, and double-hung windows. As Wetstone suggests, the intention was to be a good neighbor through literal contextualism. NHS, by contrast, has allowed Yale students greater freedom in design, and many of the eleven houses are distinctly modern in style. The change in client from Habitat for Humanity to Neighborhood Housing Services coincided with a particularly strong design faculty teaching in the Building Project studio. In 1996, during the deanship of Fred Koetter, Louise Harpman, a member of the class of 1993, began a seven-year stint as studio coordinator, joined by design critics Peggy Deamer, Brian Healy, Alan Organschi, and Turner Brooks, who was a member of the class that built the first building project, the 1967 New Zion Community Center. A few of the designs from this period, such as the 2000 house on West Read Street in the Newhallville neighborhood, strongly suggest Brooks's influence as they explored the unexpected plasticity of balloon frame construction. After leaving Yale, Harpman founded a design-build studio at the University of Texas at Austin based on Yale's program.[25]

Alan Organschi, a member of the class of 1988, currently leads the design phase of the Building Project studio, which investigates the theme of dwelling and studies examples of housing. For Organschi, what distinguishes the program today is its embrace of design innovation within tight and unforgiving, real-world constraints. Students meet the challenge of conceiving and building in a short amount of time an affordable house in an urban setting which complies with all governing building and regulatory codes, and which is nevertheless formally inventive. A lead designer of the 1986 education pavilion at Fort Nathan Hale as a student, Organschi recently observed, "It has been fascinating for me to come back to Yale and see the complexity and sophistication of the program now, how it has changed from the years when pavilions were the design problems."[26] Architect Cesar Pelli, who was dean of the School of Architecture from 1978 to 1984, expresses some regret in the change in building type, noting that many of the pavilion projects of the seventies and eighties had a freedom and exuberance—and, in some cases, a structural beauty—that may have been lost. Pelli acknowledges, however, that the social benefits to New Haven's neighborhoods more than compensate for any possible loss in design freedom that occurred when the program turned to affordable housing.[27]

James Paley, the director of the New Haven chapter of NHS for the past thirty years, admits he is sometimes surprised by the students' designs; nevertheless, he appreciates the cooperative process and attention their association with Yale has brought NHS. He points to the 2001 house on the corner of

Hallock Avenue and Fifth Street and the two adjacent houses on Parmelee Avenue and Porter Street from 2002 and 2003 as especially successful projects.[28] These three projects respond to their context through larger issues of siting, massing, and orientation, while articulating clearly modern design tropes: shed roofs, skewed walls, and oversized stock windows, combined with generously proportioned, custom glazing. Indeed, their modern vocabulary may be one of the strongest gestures they make toward revitalizing their neighborhoods, suggesting confidence in the future and in so doing conveying a spirit of optimism that reflects on their surroundings.

As the First-Year Building Project continues to evolve, the houses in New Haven may best be viewed not so much as the spirit of the sixties regained, but as the expression of a commitment to collaborative effort and social betterment that was never lost, and that has been sustained for forty years. The eighteen houses designed and constructed by Yale students since 1989 may not, in and of themselves, stabilize whole neighborhoods and revitalize the city of New Haven, but they are the building blocks of a greater society.

Endnotes

1 In a May 2006 letter to the author, Marvin Michalsen of the class of 1972 wrote, "I am struck by how much hard work was done by a lot of people with good intentions." Yale students and faculty members contributed over $600 of their own money to the community center, for example, and class member Mack Caldwell moved from New Haven to live in the housing project during the summer of 1969.

2 SENSUS, December 1970 (New Haven: Yale Arts Association) [No page].

3 Ibid. The comments pale in comparison to remarks about the faculty in another student publication of the School of Architecture, Novum Organum, December 3, 1968.

4 Ibid.

5 For Kingman Brewster, Jr., see Geoffrey Kabaservice, The Guardians: Kingman Brewster, His Circle, and the Rise of the Liberal Establishment (New York: Henry Holt and Company, Inc., 2004). For Moore, see David Littlejohn, Architect: The Life and Work of Charles W. Moore (New York: Holt Rinehart and Winston, 1984).

6 An article in the New Haven Register dated July 13, 1969, claimed there was "a bitter crisis of confidence at the school that has struck deeply at the morale of practically everyone connected with it." For the suspension of classes, see Tom Warren, "A & A Faculty Agrees to Suspend Academics" in The Yale Daily News, May 18, 1969, Vol. XC, No. 140. For the end to the City Planning program, see Kabaservice, op. cit., pp. 388–389. For the fire in the A & A Building, see Joseph Lelyveld, "After Fire, Yale Smolders" in The New York Times, June 27, 1969, p. 39, and Mark Alden Branch, "The Building That Won't Go Away" in Yale Alumni Magazine, February 1998, Vol. LXI, No.4.

7 In November 1968, Yale architecture students staged a walk-out of the annual meeting of the New England Region conference of the American Institute of Architects and went on to form The Architects Resistance in 1969.

8 Brink Thorne, letter to the author, July 2006.

9 For the Black Workshop, see "A Comprehensive Proposal for the Founding and Funding of a Black Environmentalist and Planning Establishment" in the Charles W. Moore papers, Box 8 of 17, Archives of American Art, Smithsonian Institution.

10 For the Student Community Housing Group, Inc., see "Group Urges Town, Gown Housing Units" in The New Haven Journal-Courier, March 3, 1971; "Group Seeks a New Concept in Housing for Yale Students" in The New Haven Register, March 3, 1971; and "Housing Units Ready March 1" in The New Haven Journal-Courier, February 2, 1972.

11 Robert Knight, letter to the author, May 2005.

12 Herbert S. Newman in conversation with the author, January 2006.

13 Herbert S. Newman, "First-Year Building Project: Learning Experience and Community Service" in Journal of Architectural Education, Winter 1980, Vol. 34, No. 2, p. 28.

14 Robert Works in conversation with the author, June 2006.

15 Newman, op. cit., p. 27.

16 Aaron Betsky in conversation with the author, May 2006.

17 Kay Bea Jones in conversation with the author, April 2006.

18 Marc-Antoine Laugier, Essai sur l'architecture, trans. by Wolfgang and Anni Herrmann as An Essay on Architecture (Los Angeles: Hennessey & Ingalls, 1977).

19 Robert Espejo in conversation with the author, June 2006.

20 Herbert S. Newman in conversation with the author, January 2006.

21 [No author] "The Sixteenth Annual P/A Design Awards Program" in Progressive Architecture, Vol. L, No. 1, January 1969, p. 114.

22 See Vincent Scully, American Architecture and Urbanism, (New York: Henry Holt and Company, 1988), pp. 257-269. See also Peter Katz, The New Urbanism: The Architecture of Community (New York: McGraw-Hill, 1994).

23 Michael Wetstone in conversation with the author, June 2006. Sounding a similar note, one of Wetstone's classmates, John Gilmer, stated, "Having Habitat as our client was good, in that we had to take into account the function and affordability of the house. A house is very different from a pavilion, and I think our class worked hard and took the project very seriously." Letter to the author, June 2006.

24 Paul Brouard, The Yale Building Project: A Resource Manual (New Haven: Yale School of Architecture, 1996).

25 See the website, www.designbuildtexas.com.

26 Alan Organschi in conversation with the author, August 2006.

27 Cesar Pelli in conversation with the author, July 2006.

28 James Paley in conversation with the author, June 2006.

The initial first-year building project was a community center in New Zion, a small town in east central Kentucky. Located in Jackson County about seventy miles southeast of Lexington, New Zion at the time was a loosely organized collection of houses for a few hundred people in one of the poorest regions of the state. In 1966, a group of Yale students traveled to Jackson County to do charitable and political work. They made Charles Moore aware of a local group, the New Zion Community Association, that wanted to build a community center. Composed of twenty-four families, the group raised money to purchase a half-acre site for a new building, and they agreed to sponsor what would become the first building in the forty-year and continuing history of the Yale Building Project. One of the families' main intentions was to construct a center for the youth of their community, in order to help stem the tide of young people leaving the region. Central to the program they prepared in conjunction with the Yale students was a large recreation room that could be used for basketball games, dances, meetings, and communal meals.

The students designed an almost-square building, compactly organized into served and service zones. Entered from a porch that created an open corner, a central vestibule contained a stair to the second floor and offered access to a small bathroom, a room with showers, a kitchen, and a storage alcove. These service spaces opened onto a large room intended for recreation and community meals, half the size of a basketball court. The partial second floor contained a library and a small meeting room on either side of the staircase hall, with balconies that overlooked the two-story volume of the multipurpose room. Above the library was a small loft, reached by a ladder. One notable feature of the interior was the design of a partition separating the kitchen and vestibule from the multipurpose room: the students created a series of bold "cut-out" shapes to convey a lighthearted quality. Class member Alberto Lau described this partition as "a wall full of goodies." The exterior of the building was sheathed in cedar and had a series of rooftop monitors that admitted diffused light into the interior. At the two outer corners of the multipurpose room, these monitors were triangular in shape and had both clerestories and skylights made out of translucent, corrugated fiberglass. Another triangular skylight, also in fiberglass, illuminated the staircase hall. The designers incorporated a large, exterior-mounted barn door, painted bright orange, at one corner of the basketball court to capture views across the hills and to permit cross-ventilation during the warmer months.

During the 1967 spring vacation, the entire class of thirty students participated in the construction. An initial group of eight students moved to the region to lay out the building and construct the foundation. Their classmates joined them a week later. Many students lived with local families, who prepared a buffet lunch each day at the building site. Moore and fellow faculty members Kent Bloomer and Herman Spiegel came to Appalachia for a few days, and were put to work. Most of the construction was finished in the course of this eighteen-day period, but a small crew of students returned in June to complete the building.

After serving the community for a few years, the building was vandalized and later demolished.
— Richard W. Hayes (RWH)

location: Jackson County, Kentucky
client: New Zion Community Association

project: New Zion Community Center

previous spread: The New
Zion Community Center.
top: Charles W. Moore in
Kentucky.
below: Turner Brooks and a
resident of New Zion.
opposite: Construction view.

opposite: Construction
views.
above: The completed
building.

Contacts made in Kentucky the previous year led to the building project for 1968, a community center for inhabitants of two creek banks, called Lower Grassy and Trace Branch, in Leslie County, Kentucky. Leslie County is located southeast of Jackson County, where in 1967 Yale students built the New Zion Community Center. About one hundred and fifty Leslie County families formed an association called the Lower Grassy-Trace Branch Community Development Corporation, through which they obtained funding from the U.S. Department of Housing and Urban Development to build their own community center. After seeing the building by Yale students in New Zion, they contacted Charles Moore, who decided to make this the first-year building project for the class of 1971.

The clients had a more complex program than the previous year's community center. The Lower Grassy and Trace Branch families requested the following spaces for their center: a large room that could accommodate up to two hundred people, mainly for community meals; a small meeting room; a kitchen; a clinic for a visiting nurse; an office for a VISTA worker; a classroom; a library; an indoor basketball court; and bathrooms with showers and flush toilets—rarities in this region during those years. The students suggested adding a tool shop and storage space to the program. The community group acquired a steeply sloping site located off the main road from one of the county's larger towns, Hyden.

As class member Mark Ellis described in an article published in 1968 in *Interiors* magazine, the selected design divided the program into two zones: one was public, noisy, and not always heated; the other private, quiet, and heated. The designers, led by David Shepler, combined some of the program elements to create multipurpose spaces. For example, a large, hexagonally shaped common room served alternately as basketball court and dining hall. The library was an alcove that opened off of the classroom. In Ellis's words, the design used "prismatic shapes" to articulate the separate parts of the program and to negotiate the steeply sloping site. Sheathed in vertically oriented oak siding, the 2,000-square-foot building contained four separate levels opening off a central staircase. The structure stood on a poured concrete foundation and the triangular roofs were covered in cedar shingles. Inside, the public spaces had hardwood floors and pine paneling on the walls, while private spaces had carpet and sheetrock walls.

As at New Zion, the students devised artful means to bring light into the interior. The Kentucky families were worried that vandals would destroy large expanses of glass, so the designers concealed most of the openings from the road side of the building through the use of roof monitors, clerestories, and skylights made from translucent fiberglass. Both the common room and the classroom had monitors with large clerestory windows. Two tall windows on the mountain-facing side of the building brought light to the central staircase. On opposite sides of the second-floor common room, exterior-mounted barn doors created balconies when opened, and provided cross-ventilation during the summer.

For two weeks in May, the entire class of twenty-five men and three women moved to Lower Grassy, where they lived with local families. Four students—Mark Ellis, Robert Hammell, Robert Nicolais, and David Shepler—returned to Kentucky in June and worked throughout the summer, assisted at times by Neighborhood Youth Corps boys. One condition of the HUD grant was that the community make an in-kind contribution to the effort. Consequently, local men—some of them former coal miners—helped the students build the foundation and stone retaining walls on the sloping site. Hammell recalls how "their impeccable rock-cutting skills, honed in the coal mines, enabled them to quarry native stone from a nearby creek bed. They put in long hours and built some beautiful stone walls." Interior finishing extended beyond the summer of 1968 through the fall and into the early months of 1969.

In 1991, class member Susan St. John returned to Leslie County to visit the community center, only to discover it had been demolished following a fire.
— RWH

location: Leslie County, Kentucky
client: Lower Grassy-Trace Branch Community Development Corporation

project: Lower Grassy-Trace Branch Community Center

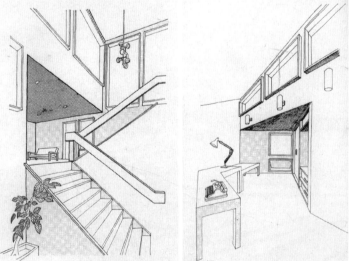

previous spread: Clerestory
window.
above: Exterior view of the
Lower Grassy-Trace Branch
Community Center.
left: Perspective sketches by
Robert Hammell.
opposite: Construction
views.

opposite: Lee Tabor and
Robert Hammell.
above: Exterior from
the rear.

In 1969, the first-year class of students worked on three different building projects: a series of recreation structures on Fishpond Lake in Whitesburg, Kentucky; a playground at Camp Cedarcrest in Orange, Connecticut; and a community center at the Long River Village housing project in Middletown, Connecticut. The previous year's project—the community center for Lower Grassy-Trace Branch in Kentucky—was a large and ambitious building, the construction of which had extended beyond the summer and into the fall semester. Charles Moore, Kent Bloomer, and Herbert Newman wanted to avoid another overrun, so they and the students found three separate, smaller projects that they estimated could be completed on time.

Dock and Floating Sculptures, Fishpond Lake, Whitesburg, Kentucky

The recreation project in Kentucky derived from contacts Moore had secured when he received a commission to design publicly-funded housing in Whitesburg, a town in the eastern corner of Kentucky near the Virginia border. Moore's firm, MLTW, designed a scheme for affordable housing for the Southeastern Kentucky Housing Development Corporation, a project that received a *Progressive Architecture* design award in 1969, but which was never built. A local anti-poverty group wanted to turn a part of the shore of a small reservoir called Fishpond Lake, located a few miles north of Whitesburg, into a recreation area. The students' design had four components: two changing rooms with walls of rough-sawn timber and cylindrical entrance towers made of concrete masonry units; a curving wood dock extending from the shore and encircling trees that stood in the water; a wood diving platform in the center of the lake; and two sculptures made out of fiberglass and Styrofoam. Painted bright, saturated colors, the free-form sculptures were designed to float on the lake while accommodating seated and reclining sunbathers. Several manufacturers donated the material for the sculptures. The diving platform, which could only be reached by swimmers or boaters, featured a one-story wood tower with a curving staircase.

Play Device, Camp Cedarcrest, Orange, Connecticut

The design for Camp Cedarcrest in Orange, Connecticut, was also like a large sculpture. Yale students designed what they called "a play machine"—an angular metal framework that held rope webbing for children to climb on, accompanied by tensile fabric enclosures, a wide slide, and groupings of tires. Founded in 1924, Camp Cedarcrest offers recreation for children from the greater New Haven area, and is supported by civic and charitable groups, including the Rotary, Lions, and Kiwanis organizations. In 1968, a team of second-year Yale students, led by class of 1970 members Michael Curtis, Daniel V. Scully, and Roc Caivano, designed and built an arts and crafts building for the camp, which is located in a wooded area five miles southwest of New Haven. The success of this project led to a second commission from the camp.

The play device designed by members of the class of 1972 was intended to improve upon the design of typical playgrounds of the time—often little more than groupings of disparate, unrelated pieces. By contrast, according to class member Marc Appleton, the architecture students conceived of the play machine as an interactive environment that experimented with different materials and forms in order to engage children's imaginations. Local manufacturers and suppliers donated all the materials. The play structure lasted only a year before being dismantled. There was an unsuccessful attempt by the City of New Haven to reconstruct it at a public beach before it was demolished.

Community Center, Long River Village, Middletown, Connecticut

The largest of the three projects was a masonry building for a community center at Long River Village in Middletown, Connecticut. Long River Village was Middletown's oldest housing project, constructed in the 1940s for temporary workers. It later housed World War II veterans and their families. Members of the class of 1972 became interested in Middletown through a studio taught by visiting critic Ray Gindroz, in which they examined ways to improve the town's main street.

locations: Whitesburg, Kentucky;
Orange, Connecticut;
Middletown, Connecticut

projects: Dock and Floating Sculptures;
Play Device, Camp Cedarcrest;
Community Center, Long River Village

previous spread: Dock and
floating sculptures in Fishpond Lake, Kentucky.
opposite: Kent Bloomer and
Mark Simon.
above: Children on the
play device.

Ironically, the building for Long River Village ended up even larger than the
1968 community center in Kentucky. A two-story structure constructed from
concrete masonry units and open web steel joists, the 4,000-square-foot building was intended to serve as both recreation center and community meeting
place. The ground floor contained a recreation room half the size of a basketball
court, and a meeting room with kitchenette and lavatories. The second floor
held a "Teen Center" overlooking the two-story volume of the recreation room
and an office for a neighborhood organization. According to lead designer
Marvin Michalsen, the design was aimed at bringing residents of the housing
project together, and so incorporated covered walkways, exterior and interior
balconies, and an exterior staircase. In its combination of primary geometric
forms with diagonal walls, the design reveals the influence of Louis I. Kahn and
Charles Moore, who had just completed a public housing project at Church
Street South in New Haven.

An architect based in Middletown, Seb Passanesi, who had previously designed
buildings for Long River Village, worked with the team of students. Class
member Mack Caldwell led the construction phase of the project and moved
from New Haven to live at Long River Village. Inexperienced in the slow pace
of masonry construction, however, the students had bit off more than they could
chew; construction extended from the summer of 1969 into the following year.
A contractor was eventually hired to finish the building, which was useable by
1971. Funding for the anticipated programs never materialized, and the building
lasted only a short time before being demolished. In 1999, all of the remaining
buildings at Long River Village were demolished.
— RWH

above: Interior view of
the community center in
Middletown, Connecticut.
right: Interior and exterior
views of the community
center.

In 1970, first-year students designed and built a cabin and a barn addition for the Mayhew Program, a charitable organization that runs a camp for adolescent boys on an island in Newfound Lake in New Hampshire. Located in the middle of the state, north of the town of Bristol, Mayhew Island is about fifty-five acres in size, and can only be reached by boat. Started in 1969, the Mayhew Program developed out of summer camp on the island originally maintained by the Groton School, a preparatory school in Massachusetts.

The project was divided into two phases. During the first phase, the entire class traveled to the island for two weeks during the spring 1970 term to build a series of additions to an existing barn intended to transform it into a recreation pavilion. The interventions included opening up one wall with a large window to take advantage of a view of the water, and transforming another wall into an operable drawbridge. The students designed and painted large lettering in the style of supergraphics used by Charles Moore in many of his own buildings. According to Kent Bloomer, who secured the commission from the Mayhew Program's board of directors, the project had "a bit of a scattershot program with a little here and there" and the students also built foundations for some of the camp's tent structures on the island.

The second phase of the project took place during the summer after the end of classes, and seven students—Judy Bing, Nancy Monroe, Tom Doremus, Joe Ford, Martin Hoffmeister, Kiran Shankar, and Robert J. "Buzz" Yudell—lived on the island and built a cabin for the camp director. Called "The North Cabin," the hexagonal building had a shed roof inspired by the Sea Ranch Condominiums in Gualala, California, designed by Moore's firm, MLTW. The students constructed a box-beam truss out of plywood to support the roof. The cabin served as the director's residence for a few years and is now used as a dormitory for senior camp counselors.

The students mastered the difficulties of living on an island with no running water and where all provisions had to be ferried by boat from the mainland. One of their first tasks was resuscitating a submerged lifeboat that they christened the "Lusitania." They also built a raft to transport lumber and large supplies, including a gas generator they used to power their saw. During the summer, each took a turn as camp cook, preparing the communal meals on a wood-burning stove. Nancy Monroe remembers that when Charles Moore visited, he slept in a sleeping bag on the porch of the building the students occupied. "He kept a miniature comb in his sleeping bag and each morning combed his mustache with it," she recalls. Buzz Yudell observed that the experience of living on an uninhabited island had "both a Robinson Crusoe quality and inevitable *Lord of the Flies* moments." Such primitive living conditions were a challenge for the group. Nevertheless, as Tom Doremus recalls, "We all had a lot of laughs." — RWH

opposite: Thomas Doremus, Nancy Monroe, and Judy Bing on Mayhew Island.

1970

location: Newfound Lake, New Hampshire
client: The Mayhew Program

project: Cabin and Recreation Structure on Mayhew Island

In 1971, a series of small structures were built at Jacob's Beach, the public beach in Guilford, Connecticut, about ten miles east of New Haven. Although their clients presumed that a single building would emerge from the process, the class ended up breaking their design into parts and scattering them across the breadth of the beach — their intention being to reduce the scale of the architecture and preserve the natural setting. All of the structures have since been demolished.

Jacob's Beach is a crescent of flat sand one hundred yards deep and a few hundred yards wide, bounded by shoreline residences on the west, and fields of tall marsh grasses in all other directions. An unpaved road leads to a gravel parking lot behind it. For several years the town had considered renovating and expanding an existing bathroom at the beach, but the anticipated costs were too high. A member of Guilford's Recreation and Parks Commission had heard of the Yale Building Project and its donated design and construction services, and thought the program might present a means of reducing costs to levels acceptable to the town's board of selectmen. The Commission approached Yale faculty member Kent Bloomer, who was also a Guilford resident, and a deal was struck.

Students were asked to renovate the existing bathrooms, add spaces for vending machines and changing rooms, and provide a shelter for beachgoers. The presumption was that all of these elements would be incorporated into the existing building, but in an effort to avoid monumentality and to foreground the natural setting, the design program was broken into thirds. The two largest structures — the sun-and-wind shelter and the bathrooms — were placed at the east and west edges of the beach, away from the surf and near the parking lot. A boardwalk connected them. At its midpoint where most visitors would step onto the sand, the students placed the changing rooms, the only interruption to the overall view.

The changing rooms, a group of six portable boxes clad in diagonal cedar boards, were each approximately four feet square and seven feet tall. Two sported decorative, crescent-shaped tops described by class members alternately as "Viking horns" or "Choctaw fertility symbols," whimsical flourishes intended to mark entry points to the beach. Even though they were placed discreetly at its far edges, they were still prominent enough to attract public attention — not always positive, causing some longtime residents of the beach access road, Seaside Avenue, to write letters to the local paper complaining about the students' design.

From the changing rooms, the boardwalk led west to the restrooms and vending machines, and east to the sun and wind shelter. To take advantage of the existing plumbing connection, the new restroom facility was erected on the same spot as the original bathroom. The new design had a minimalist, prismatic form: two shed roofs rising toward one another, with one side pushed higher to create a southern-facing, open clerestory. Geometric voids punched into the vertical cedar siding — an archway, a large circle, and two rectangular recesses — created not only an abstract, formal composition, but provided access to the building's services.

In contrast, the sun and wind shelter at the other end of the beach, though still somewhat geometrically fixed in plan, unfolded gradually, its walls behaving like shutters. The structure was a simple wooden platform at its core, with a gable roof for shade. Cedar-clad walls placed outside the roof's perimeter were rotated forty-five degrees from the structure's main axis, forming a series of boat-like prows. The designers' intent was to break the wind without interrupting the view, providing a sense of enclosure while maintaining a connection to the beach. As a final gesture, they cut a large circle like a porthole into one of the walls, echoing the restroom's circular cut-out at the opposite end of the boardwalk.
— Ted Whitten (TW)

location: Jacobs Beach, Guilford, Connecticut

client: Town of Guilford

project: Sun Shelter, Bathrooms, and Changing Rooms

previous spread: Exterior
view of the beach pavilion.
above: Exterior view of the
changing rooms.
left: Kent Bloomer and
students.
opposite: The changing
rooms and parking lot.

left: Exterior view.
right: Local press coverage.

Architecture Students Design and Build Beach Pavilions

"Instead of dominating the beach, we chose to embrace it," said Diane Blitzer, one of the 19 Yale architecture students who designed and constructed a three-section beach house in Guilford, Conn., this past summer. Using donated materials and their own labor, the students saved the town several thousand dollars and fostered good town-gown relations (Guilford is a suburb of New Haven). The young designers eschewed "monumental" buildings, erecting instead a discreet set of buildings to fit in with the low-lying landscape.

SHOWER IN THE SUNSHINE at the new bath houses on Jacobs Beach gives big sister a chance to wash the salt and sand off from the boys who have been swimming.

In 1972, the Building Project undertook an ambitious renovation of the interior of the Wallingford, Connecticut, train station, as part of a community effort to save the historic building from demolition and to provide space for social services.

Wallingford, one of Connecticut's oldest towns, is located on a ridge overlooking the Quinnipiac River Valley, the main transportation and shipping route between New Haven, Hartford, and points north. Although the original Main Street retains its quaint, well-heeled air, the Valley – always utilitarian – has suffered the vagaries of changing technologies, economies, and demographics.

The train station, built in 1871 for the New York, New Haven, and Hartford Railroad (NY, NH & H Railroad), is a one-story, red brick depot with a slate mansard roof and curving iron brackets. By the late 1960s, with the diminishing popularity of rail travel, the railroad could no longer maintain the building. Although many stations along the NY, NH & H were demolished in this period, at the prodding of a small group of residents, the town bought the station in order to preserve it.

Students from a local trade school, along with other volunteers, worked to clean up the building, but the effort lagged. In early 1972, an article appeared in the *New Haven Sunday Register* about the fledgling Yale Building Project and the program's work at Jacob's Beach. One of the volunteers sent the article to the Mayor, hoping to spur him into action. The Mayor did indeed contact Yale, and the town subsequently appropriated money for the station's clean-up and renovation.

The town wanted spaces for community meetings, a senior center, band-practice facilities for the local fife and drum corps, an after-school club for teens, and daycare facilities. It was still a working station, so the renovation also required a downsized ticket booth, railroad office, and direct access to the train platform from the front door. The winning design guts the interior and opens up full-height spaces at either end of the structure. Offices and meeting rooms are grouped at the center and in the basement. At the public entrance on the north end, a geometric system of stairs and ramps fills the tall space, forming an expansive, helix-like triangle that serves as the building's main vertical circulation. From these central stairs, a ramp leads to a large, multipurpose room occupying the second story and former attic. The ceiling is articulated by the attic's old mansard roof, and its original floor timbers are left intact. The full-height space at the south end of the station is even more dramatic. Each of the three red brick stories is ringed with windows, filling the open volume with light. The students floated a few old timbers in the space, clipped and hanging, as reminders of the original structure.

The construction proved very difficult. One hundred years of coal dust had accumulated on the interior surfaces, so the students spent days simply cleaning brick and removing waste. During this work it became apparent that the multipurpose space did not have enough headroom. They drew up plans to lower the existing second floor eighteen inches. To accomplish this they had to cut large timber beams, lower them with a pulley and chain system, and reset them on new steel brackets – a process that brought up concerns about the lateral stability of the station's old brick bearing walls. Herman Spiegel, a structural engineering professor at the School of Architecture, was consulted, and a shoring system was developed to hold the walls in place while construction proceeded. By the end of the school year, the renovation was far from complete. A crew of students joined by local volunteers and trade school students stayed to work throughout the summer and much of the following year.

The project has been in active use ever since. In the early 1990s, the town of Wallingford appropriated several hundred thousand dollars to renovate the building's exterior. The interior spaces were left intact.

— TW

location: Wallingford, Connecticut
client: Town of Wallingford

project: Renovation of the Wallingford Train Station

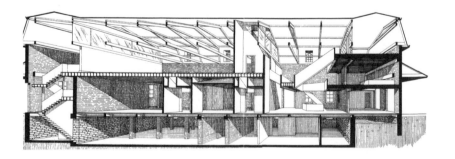

previous spread: The
Wallingford Train Station.
above: Gordon Black.
left: Section perspective.
opposite: Interior view.

The 1973 building project — a large open pavilion at Camp Farnam, a country retreat for city kids — would be the first of three at this woodsy site (see 1974 and 1976). The camp is a satellite of the Farnam Neighborhood House, a youth center in the Fair Haven section of New Haven. Located in Durham, Connecticut, a sparsely populated farming community in the rolling hills south of Hartford, the camp is an ad hoc collection of small clapboard buildings, a pool, and a basketball court set on a high, wooded bluff overlooking a pond.

The pavilion is at the center of the camp, marking and enclosing the intersection of paths linking the various buildings and activities. Placed against a rocky wall, it has an eye-catching scale and sculptural presence that resonates with the craggy landscape, giving the scattered buildings a focus and architectural identity.

The structure is composed of two identical shed roofs placed several feet apart and rotated in plan one hundred and eighty degrees, so that the high point of one aligns with the low point of the other. The roof system reaches across the space between the sheds, resulting in the rafters forming a spiral pattern in section. Originally, this portion of the roof was finished with translucent material.

The building uses a field of eighteen-foot equilateral triangles to generate its plan. The pattern is expressed by expansion joints traced in the concrete slab, as well as by its unusual perimeter. Where needed, columns spring from the points of the triangles. The space under the twisting roof — the area between the rotated sheds — acts as an aisle marking the path from the swimming pool to the basketball courts. This path was later blocked at one end by a fireplace built by the 1974 building project team.

The volume of each shed is built from three large triangular trusses, thirty-six feet long and twelve feet high. One of the three trusses is exposed at the edge of the building and forms a façade of sorts, a natural entry point. The other two trusses are set within the building, joined at their tall edges and radiating out in line with the triangular pattern below. All structural members are constructed of built-up standard dimensional lumber, and the roof is sheathed with plywood covered in asphalt shingles.

For students just finishing their first year of architecture school, shady Camp Farnam was a perfect summer retreat. Alumnus Carl Pucci, for example, remembers working on the roof, perched among tree branches in the dappled sunlight, the pond shimmering below him. The following year, he and a few classmates, none of whom had prior experience in construction, built a windmill at Kent Bloomer's house as an independent study project. Pucci credits his Building Project experience with giving him the confidence to build the windmill, and later to experiment with unusual details and materials in practice.
— TW

location: Durham, Connecticut
client: Farnam Neighborhood House

project: Pavilion, Camp Farnam

previous spread: Interior
view of the pavilion at
Camp Farnam.
opposite: Interior view of
the roof structure.
above: Exterior view.

In 1974, students built three projects: an experimental "black box" theater at Trumbull College, one of Yale's residential colleges, in New Haven; two fireplaces and a landscape terrace addition to the pavilion at Camp Farnam in Durham, Connecticut (the 1973 building project); and a playground for disabled children in Hamden, Connecticut.

Theater

Nicholas Chapel Theater, known to students at Yale College as Nick Chapel, was located in a former squash court in the sub-basement of Trumbull College, and existed until the college was renovated in the summer of 2005. A typical squash court, the space was two stories high, with a door at the back and a viewing balcony above. The 1974 theater design reversed the action, placing the stage at the back of the squash court, and taking advantage of the balcony for a fly space, and the door for an entrance to stage right. Students added a second door at stage left by cutting through the existing masonry wall, and in so doing had to remove one hundred bags of rubble, carrying them up two flights of stairs to the street.

For audience seating, students designed a "pipe and joint" system to create a series of demountable platforms that could be arranged at the pleasure of the actors. Chairs were purchased from a used furniture shop, their legs removed and pipes mounted to their seats, allowing them to lock into the pipe structure. A series of wood panels about two by four feet, with steel tabs at the edges, were set into the pipe assembly to create aisles and footrests. Salvaged doors were mounted on the walls with swivels to create moveable acoustic baffles.

In its thirty years of existence, Nick Chapel was a beloved home for multitudes of Yale undergraduate productions, so much so that it became the inspiration for similar theaters in other Yale residential colleges. Scenery was painted directly onto the walls, which were repainted black after each run. After about twenty years of weekly productions, the layers of paint grew so deep that the stage doors stopped functioning, even trapping one actor on stage during a performance. Students also painted the names of their productions onto the halls surrounding the theater. The result, after three decades, was an explosion of graffiti.

Fireplaces and Landscape Terrace

In 1974, students also added two fireplaces and a stone terrace to the Camp Farnam pavilion in Durham, Connecticut, the previous year's building project. They embedded the first fireplace in a steep hill rising at the edge of the pavilion where the roof is low. Its heavy stone masonry emerges from the hill and spreads under the canopy. Three brick arches, about three feet high, form the openings to the hearth, flush with the pavilion floor. The students piled large, round stones on the three arches to form the body of the fireplace and chimney, giving it a squat, conical form akin to Native American construction seen hundreds of years earlier in this area. At the rear, the masonry spreads across the steep hillside to form terraced retaining walls and a stone patio.

Pressed into the fireplace's thick mortar joints are tiny sculptures of eyes, noses, lips, and fingers by Jim Kessler, an architecture student and sculptor. Kessler had applied to do an MFA at Yale, but his application was accidentally put into the architecture school file. As the story goes, after he was admitted to the architecture school — and when it became apparent that he wouldn't be admitted to the sculpture program — he changed careers. Today he is a designer for HOK in Washington, D.C. The sculptures were intended to charm young campers, but barely survived the design review. To the camp's founder and benefactor, who was a survivor of World War I, the sculptures looked like tiny body parts protruding from rubble, as if trapped. Aware that such historical allusions would be lost on small children, however, he approved the design.

The second fireplace is more modern. Built from brick, it sprawls to fill a bay of the pavilion, corbelling upward in an open pyramid topped by a metal flue.

locations: New Haven, Connecticut;
Durham, Connecticut;
Hamden, Connecticut

projects: Nicholas Chapel Theater, Trumbull College, Yale;
Two Fireplaces at Camp Farnam;
Playground at The Unitarian Society of New Haven

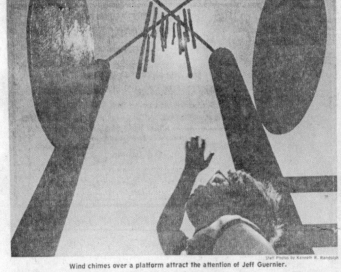

Staff Photos by Kenneth R. Randolph

Wind chimes over a platform attract the attention of Jeff Guernier.

Just For Fun

The students at the Elizabeth Ives School in Hamden have an exciting playground, and their parents have some money left in their playground fund. And that makes everyone happy.

The playground was designed and built by students from the Yale School of Architecture. The parents set a $1,000 limit, and the job was done for less than $800.

Designing the playground presented several problems, said Mrs. Betty Sword, director of the Ives School. The students have emotional problems and-or neurological impairment which either causes or complicates their ability to learn. The children range in age from 3 to 12, so a variety of abilities had to be considered.

Contact was made with the architecture school, and the playground design was taken on as a class project.

Now the playground is a maze of telephone poles, platforms,

The telephone poles are different heights to allow children of different ages and abilities to climb and jump off. There are platforms to run across or to sit under where children can find a quiet spot to be by themselves. They can also crawl on a mesh of macramed ropes which are strung from a platform and anchored to the ground. There is a merry-go-round, a sandbox and lots of old tires for climbing on. There are even brick paths which lead children to different play areas.

WESTBROOK WOMEN

The third annual arts and crafts festival sponsored by the Women's Club of Westbrook will be held on June 22 from 10 a.m. to 6 p.m. The event will be held on the ground of the town hall and the firehouse. In case of rain, the festival will be held on June 29. The public is

The playground keeps students in action.

previous spread: One of the fireplaces at Camp Farnam.
opposite: Barry Svigals in the squash court at Trumbull College.
above: Newspaper article on the playground at the Elizabeth Ives School.

The hearth is raised and open on all sides. Kessler's sculptures are here confined to low limestone masonry walls set within the orthogonal pattern of the mortar joints.

Playground

First-year students also designed and built a playground at the Unitarian Society of New Haven, located in Hamden, Connecticut. The project was for students attending the Elizabeth Ives School, a private school for children with a variety of mild disabilities, most frequently autism. At the time, the school occupied part of the Unitarian Society's building.

In a creative interplay of materials and structure, the class designed a jungle gym comprised of salvaged telephone poles, wood-plank walkways, rubber tires, and rope ladders topped off with a set of wind chimes. Rather than design an object with a clear formal identity, the students based their concept on the ways the children might use a playground, paying special attention to their developmental limitations. A series of pathways and enclosures was created, allowing Elizabeth Ives students to explore a variety of experiences and relationships within the protected confines of the playground. The school raised $1,000 for the project, but the students delivered it for $800.

The playground was demolished in 2002, when the school moved.
— TW

In 1975, first-year students worked on two vastly different projects: a large health center for the West Virginia community of Cabin Creek, and a small project for an individual client in Branford, Connecticut. The Cabin Creek Medical Center is the largest of the building projects and the only health facility so far in the program's history. It is also the last of the building projects in Appalachia.

Cabin Creek Health Center

Yale students learned of the need for the community clinic through a member of the class of 1977, Jonathan Kammel, whose cousin worked for an anti-poverty group in this coal-mining region of West Virginia after graduating from Wesleyan University. The Cabin Creek Health Association was established in the 1970s by the United Mine Workers of America to offer health care to miners infected with black lung disease (pneumoconiosis). The Association wanted to build a community health center that would offer both health services and educational programs for the rural and impoverished region. They secured funding for the project through a $75,000 loan from the United Mine Workers and a grant from the Claude Worthington Benedum Foundation, a Pittsburgh-based charity that supports community development in West Virginia and southwestern Pennsylvania. Once contact with the Yale School of Architecture was established, Craig Robinson, a member of the non-profit Cabin Creek Health Association and now the executive director of the Cabin Creek Medical Center, became the liaison on the project. A former VISTA volunteer, Robinson and two coal miners traveled to New Haven for the final design reviews during the spring 1975 semester.

Cabin Creek is a small town southeast of Charleston, in the Kanawha River Valley, a region with a long history of coal mining. The building site was actually in Dawes, a hamlet six miles south of Cabin Creek. Class member Barbara Flanagan described the immediate surroundings as "shacks along a road that dead-ended at a coal mine. It looked like nothing we'd seen before. The region's poverty put design in a different light." Located adjacent to the creek, the site was within a floodplain. Consequently, before Yale students arrived, the Army Corps of Engineers dredged the site and installed earthen fill so that a block foundation could be built. During the late spring of 1975, about thirty members of the first-year class moved to West Virginia, where they stayed for five weeks in a dormitory at Morris Harvey College in Charleston, a half-hour drive from Dawes. Paul Brouard lived with the students during the entire period, and faculty members Herbert Newman and George Buchanan visited during the early summer.

The plan of the selected design derived from the site and the program, which is organized into three elements: an entrance unit composed of a porte cochere and a waiting area with a high ceiling and exposed wood framing; one linear wing containing administration offices and examination rooms; and a second, compact wing with an on-site laboratory. Three large light monitors bring copious amounts of daylight to the interior and give the exterior a public scale. The wood-frame building is sheathed in unpainted, tongue-in-groove cedar. According to Calvert Bowie, a member of the original design team, the distinctive lettering on the street side of the porte cochere was based on art deco buildings the team had observed in downtown Charleston while living at Morris Harvey College. Yale students finished the outer shell by the end of the summer and local workers completed the interior finishes after the students left.

As class member Kevin Lichten recalled, the project was notable for the logistical challenges involved in building a 7,500-square-foot-structure in an isolated region, five hundred miles from New Haven. A local architect, Tag Galyean, who also ran the region's Cadillac dealership, was hired to help with the Kanawha County agencies. For class member Eric Epstein, who entered graduate school with no background in architecture, the project "really grounded me. It was such a direct experience; you'll never forget what it's like trying to carry a twenty-foot-long two-by-twelve." Working and living so far from home in such different circumstances created a unique social experience for a group of first-year students from diverse backgrounds. Kammel remembers in particular the heartfelt efforts by local families to welcome the students: "They really took us in. We got

locations: **Dawes, West Virginia;**
Branford, Connecticut
clients: **Cabin Creek Health Association;**
Private Client

projects: **Cabin Creek Medical Center;**
House Addition

previous spread: Graham
Williams standing atop the
roof trusses.
above: Louise Braverman
and Stephen Tolkin.
opposite top: Construction
view.
opposite bottom: The
building near completion.
overleaf: Signage at the
porte cochere.

to see how people were living, which made the whole project resonate as an experience." The importance of the health center to the community was unmistakable; they followed the progress of the construction on a daily basis.

The building is still in use as a community health center and director Robinson describes it as "a highly functional building." It has been expanded and renovated, and the exterior siding has been painted. Class member Laura Lintz returned to Cabin Creek in 1985, and was given a tour by staff, during which she was happy to see the interiors flooded with daylight from the roof monitors.

Private House Addition
Four members of the first-year class had ties to the New Haven area that prevented their moving to West Virginia for the summer. Instead, they worked on a small project for a private client in Branford. The owner of a heating and cooling business needed additions to his office and house. The students designed the commercial addition, the main feature of which was a solar heating system, but did not build it themselves. They did, however, spend the summer of 1975 building their design for a two-story addition to the owner's house.
— RWH

In 1976, the Building Project was scheduled to return to West Virginia to design a building for Cabin Creek Quilts, a small collective of women who make and sell original quilts. Students went through the traditional Building Project design process, choosing teams and producing multiple designs. A review was held and a winner chosen, but a week before the class was to travel to West Virginia the project's financing fell through — partly due to controversy over the winning design. In an attempt to revive the project, Paul Brouard and a group of students visited the clients at their own expense, but to no avail.

Instead, the Project returned for the third time to Camp Farnam in Durham, Connecticut (see 1973 and 1974), where they were commissioned to build three cabins for overnight campers. Because time was short, the class simply divided into three groups, with each group working independently on a cabin. There was a day of desk design, and then construction began — details were worked out in the field in a true design-build process. An energetic competition developed between teams during the construction phase, as each raced to complete its project ahead of and more inventively than the others.

The three cabins are located across a basketball court from the 1973 pavilion several yards into the woods. Each cabin measures about twenty by twenty feet and is perched on posts three feet above grade. Each has similar massing, a roof with deep eaves, and uses naturally finished, horizontal flush boards for cladding and shutters. The cabins are arranged on a hill about forty feet apart in a line running southwest to northeast. The hill descends steeply to a pond belonging to the camp. To stretch their budget, students salvaged materials from local junkyards, including recycled telephone poles, which were used as part of all three structures.

Cabin One, the lowest, is the only one without a light scoop reminiscent of Charles Moore's California Houses. Instead, it looks to Louis Kahn's Trenton Bathhouse for its inspiration, as well as to the Far East, expressing an austere Japanese sensibility. The plan is a square with its corners cut away, where telephone poles placed outside of the building, but still within the implied square, provide the vertical structure. Its hipped roof is a four-sided pyramid with deep eaves and a shallow pitch, and its interior, like those of the other two cabins, is a single, unfinished bunk room.

Cabin Two is structured in part by four posts that sit well inside the building, rising from grade through the floor and up to a large light scoop facing southwest toward Cabin One. The posts form a seven-by-seven-foot square around which four rectangular spaces pinwheel, containing the bunks and the entry at the western corner. The bunk areas are raised a step, making the plan's central square a recessed "gathering space." At the foundation, long diagonal members reach from the bases of each post to the edges of the building, reflecting the roof form and giving the cabin a crystalline appearance.

Cabin Three, at the top of the hill, has a straightforward rectangular plan with the long axis aligned with the siting of the other cabins. At the entry on the long northwest face, the door is inset a few feet. In response, the opposite back wall bumps out. The section of roof above it continues and completes the gesture, gathering itself into a light scoop located directly above the front door. It has the same dimensions as that on the roof of Cabin Two, but faces in the opposite direction.
— TW

1976

location: Durham, Connecticut
client: Farnam Neighborhood House

project: Three Cabins at Camp Farnam

previous spread: One of
the three cabins at Camp
Farnam.
opposite and above:
Construction views.

In 1977, students designed and built a large pavilion at Camp Laurelwood, a residential summer camp for Jewish children. Doubling as a roof for a basketball court and an outdoor theater, the project was challenging programmatically and structurally due to its large scale and long spans.

Camp Laurelwood is a small campus of clapboard cabins, mess halls, and activity buildings hidden in the rocky, wooded hills of North Madison, twenty miles east of New Haven. The building project site is located beyond a rise at the edge of the camp and consists of two side-by-side, full basketball courts, and a large playground beyond.

The pavilion is tall and airy, and covers the court closest to camp. Low volumes with shed roofs line the two walls facing the camp, mediating the change in scale from the residential buildings to the large, roofed space above the court. On the far side, the volume is open to the adjacent open-air court and playground.

The court roof is a single gable framed in a close-set lattice of trusses, and covered with translucent, corrugated fiberglass panels. The trusses spring from twenty-foot-tall columns, lifting them safely beyond the reach of a bouncing ball. Above twelve feet, the columns are stabilized by a continuous box beam that rings the space. Two-by-four framing between the columns is sheathed with plywood, locking the four walls together and making them behave as a structural unit. Once the columns were in place and stabilized by the structural "ring," twelve-by-fifty-foot sections of roof were constructed on the ground, and then lifted into place by a crane.

Initially, the designers planned a formally expressive, opaque roof. But Richard Kelly, the renowned lighting designer who worked for Louis Kahn on the Yale Art Gallery and the Yale Center for British Art, and who was a visiting lecturer at the architecture school at the time, pointed out that the scheme would not provide enough light for basketball. The challenge, he said, would be to provide diffuse, natural light while diminishing the sun's glare, especially since basketball players spend much of their time looking upward. On his advice, the designers abandoned the complex roof they had been laboring over and replaced it with the simple translucent roof that was ultimately built.

On the sides of the building closest to camp, the large central space is surrounded by the lower secondary volumes cut into the descending hillside. Along the court's baseline, an elongated shed roof forms the entry, and a colonnade provides passage to the open-air court and playground. On the long side of the court, two low, shed-roofed volumes are plugged into the column bays to form a stage and dressing room. The stage opens onto the central space at mid-court, turning it into a theater.

The building is clad in painted plywood. The low shed volumes have thin, shallow eaves, resulting in minimal, taut, and prismatic masses reminiscent of Charles Moore's work of the 1960s and '70s. The roof of the large gabled space, however, has a shallow pitch and extended eaves with exposed rafter tails. This, with the translucent corrugated roofing common to agricultural buildings, suggests a vernacular barn or warehouse, making for an unexpected juxtaposition of style and type.
— TW

location: North Madison, Connecticut
client: Camp Laurelwood

project: Basketball Court Roof at Camp Laurelwood

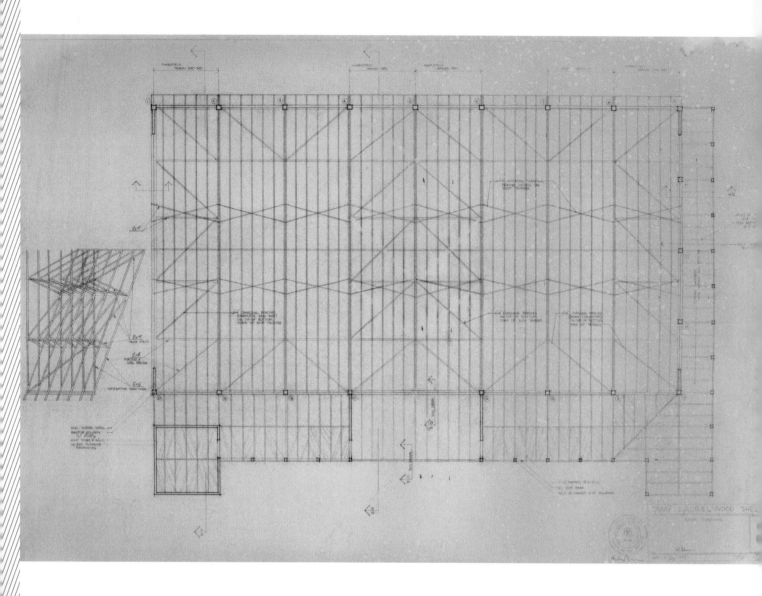

previous spread: Interior
view of the basketball court
at Camp Laurelwood.
opposite: Plan of the roof
structure.
above and right: Interior
and exterior views.

In 1978, the class of 1980 designed and built an outdoor pavilion at the Stratford Festival Theatre in Stratford, Connecticut. Stratford is ten miles west of New Haven at the juncture of the Housatonic River and Long Island Sound. The theater is on the west bank of the river, about a mile inland from the Sound in a low-lying area with long views of water, marshes, and marinas. It was built by the State of Connecticut in 1955, in part to celebrate the town's British namesake, and the work of its most famous resident. Until closing in the late 1990s, the theater hosted the nationally recognized American Shakespeare Festival that featured actors like Katherine Hepburn and Christopher Plummer, among many others. The town is currently working to revive the festival and renovate the theater.

The theater is a bulky structure somewhat reminiscent of the original Globe Theater in London that expresses its program in its massing: a several-story-tall rectangular volume containing the stage and fly space is set next to a lower volume holding the seating. Both volumes are clad in vertical teak boards painted gray. Outdoor walkways leading from the theater entrance to the mezzanine seating hang from the angled walls of the auditorium. Although the theater is surrounded by a lawn where patrons picnic before shows, or congregate during intermissions, the building itself provides little space for these activities.

The students were asked to design an outdoor pavilion that would link to the theater and serve as a gathering area and snack bar during performances. At other times, it would operate as a stage for smaller outdoor productions. The winning design developed by Robert Kahn and Reese Owens, an unusually small team, was organized around the concept of the "proscenium," the wall through which the stage protrudes in a traditional theater, and played with ideas of stage vs. backstage, inside vs. out, actor vs. audience. The design started with a traditionally detailed band shell or gazebo of the sort one finds on town greens in New England. Bisecting this and forming the east wall of the pavilion was a lattice — a screen of diagonal wood strips — rendered, like the gazebo, in a form derived from historicist garden designs. Highly untraditional, however, was the lattice's large scale and flat, two-dimensional appearance, both of which announced the wall's conceptual intent: to act as a proscenium, dividing audience from performance.

The architecture made this relationship more complex, however, for on this stage the audience and the performance could be on either side of the proscenium. From the gazebo, performers could face outward, with the audience on the lawn and the pavilion serving as backstage; or, the performers could face into the pavilion, with the audience under the roof and on a balcony (although the balcony was not completed). Most often, the pavilion was simply used as shelter during intermissions of performances in the main theater. Even in this case, the concept of the "stage" still resonated, as patrons spent the break from the performance in another performance space.

The pavilion was supported on four roof trusses set on deep truss columns, all built up from standard-size lumber. Bracing was provided by purlins at the roof and tensioned steel rods between the columns. A balcony intended to link to the suspended walkways on the main theater was built, but the connection was never completed, nor guardrails installed. Fieldstone pavers were used as ground cover, and the structure was roofed in striped canvas. A freestanding, U-shaped snack bar at the north end was clad in clear-finished vertical boards.

The waterfront site, rehearsals in the theater, and the close-knit construction crew made for a fun summer, recall alumni. The students' picnics and soccer games held on the large lawn led to requests for quiet from the producers of *As You Like It*, which starred the actress Lynn Redgrave. The completion of the pavilion was celebrated by a party and concert that featured the jazz musician Lionel Hampton.
— TW

previous spread: The
picnic pavilion at the
Stratford Festival Theatre.
above and opposite:
Construction views.

The 1979 building project was an addition to and renovation of a building at the West Haven Community House (WHCH), a private charity with programs for troubled teens, daycare, pregnancy support, and adults with mental retardation. The project is notable for its large scale, use of masonry, and engagement with social issues, unusual during this period of the Project.

The Community House is located on a busy street in West Haven, a gritty, blue-collar city just west of New Haven. Founded in 1941, the center's original buildings consisted of a large Victorian house and a carriage house on a long, narrow lot.

In the 1970s the Community House needed to expand, as demand for its programs grew. The director pitched the project to Yale as a way of motivating his board of directors to raise the funds needed for expansion. He had to pitch the project to the architecture students as well, since during this period building projects were typically open-air structures like picnic pavilions and outdoor stages. The winning scheme was the only one that proposed keeping the existing carriage house, a source of controversy for the students. Some saw the approach as overly nostalgic. However, the winning team recognized the sentimental value the building had to the client, and successfully integrated it into their program. The resulting building starts with the carriage house, and then extrudes back from it along the long axis of the site, tripling its size. The new portion is two stories, sunken a half story below grade to match the ridge height of the carriage house.

On the interior of the new area there are two stories of multipurpose rooms with long ramps for accessible circulation, a novel design for the time before the Americans with Disabilities Act made ramps commonplace. The carriage house was refinished as a single, large space with exposed timbers. The entrance is located at the juncture of the new and old structures within a smaller day-lit volume marked by a large crescent-shaped opening in the shingle roof, exposing the steady rhythm of rafters running beneath.

The construction quickly became a struggle. The carriage house needed a new foundation, so the building was jacked up, the earth beneath excavated, and a new foundation poured. Because the building would house people with disabilities, officials required a high standard of fire resistance. Thus, the design was changed to masonry and a firewall required to rise above the roof was added between the carriage house and the new areas. A retired mason was hired to work with the students, and in the course of the project over seven thousand concrete masonry units were laid. In the end, a large group of students had to stay for the summer to complete the work, requiring a round of emergency fundraising.

Although the decorative roof over the entrance is now gone, the work of the project has been long-lasting, as the building remains in heavy use.
— TW

location: West Haven, Connecticut
client: West Haven Community House

project: Addition and Renovation, West Haven Community House

1979

previous spread: Entrance
to the West Haven
Community House.
above and opposite:
Construction views.

In 1980, students designed and built a 4,300-square-foot structure at Camp Sequassen, a Boy Scout camp in New Hartford (formerly Winsted), Connecticut. Called the Cohen Memorial Lodge, the building consists of two wings, one of which is a dormitory that houses twenty-four beds, the other a nature and conservation center. The lodge accommodates year-round activities for the Connecticut Yankee Council of the Boy Scouts of America, such as winter retreats and small conferences, as well as summer camping.

Constructed on a sloping, wooded site, the design divides the program into two separate enclosures standing on a raised wood platform. Approached from the higher side of the site, a gently raked ramp leads to a central courtyard or piazza-like space from which each wing is entered. The two volumes are connected by a continuous hip roof that extends across the entrance side of the courtyard. On the opposite side, the site drops more than five feet, and the wood platform, resting on concrete sonotube supports, becomes a balcony from which to view the wooded hills. While the lodge appears symmetrical from the entrance side, the deck is actually L-shaped, since one corner of the nature center is cut back, creating an opening that frames the landscape. Both volumes are clad in vertical tongue-in-groove cedar siding with horizontal cedar siding on the interiors. Within the simple and elegant composition, subtle details differentiate the two volumes: for example, the nature center has two exterior-mounted barn doors as its entrance, and the dormitory, a cruciform arrangement of windows and a single door.

According to class member William Sherman, the design derived from an analysis of barns and the architecture of wood churches — particularly their expansive interior volumes and tall, peaked roofs. The students based their design for the twenty-four bunk beds in the dormitory wing on horse stalls. In contrast to typical barns, however, the lodge is constructed as a stick frame using dimension lumber, instead of as a timber building with post and beam construction. The class sought to avoid having to bring a crane to the sloping and isolated site, so they bolted two-by-ten-inch joists together to support the commodious roof, which reaches a height of twenty feet above the platform. A band of translucent fiberglass sheathing inserted near the peak of the roof introduces daylight into the two wings, accentuating the diagonal bracing of the structure.

The entire class started construction during the spring semester, but a core group stayed on through the summer of 1980 to complete the building. While some students commuted from New Haven, about forty miles south of New Hartford, most of the construction team lived in cabins at the camp. Kay Bea Jones recalls that "the landscape setting in the hills outside Winsted was glorious — we had canoes and swam after each day's work. Laboring in the woods with my classmates was great fun; we ate and drank well too." For Tom Kligerman, the setting and the communal meals contributed to a memorable experience: "Winsted was an amazingly beautiful place to work. Student volunteers made dinner each night. I made an incredibly hot chili that I am still embarrassed about."

Although requiring maintenance over the years, the lodge remains one of the most popular buildings at the six-hundred-acre camp.
— Marissa Brown (MB) and RWH

location: New Hartford (formerly Winsted), Connecticut
client: The Connecticut Yankee Council of the Boy Scouts of America

project: Cohen Memorial Lodge at Camp Sequassen

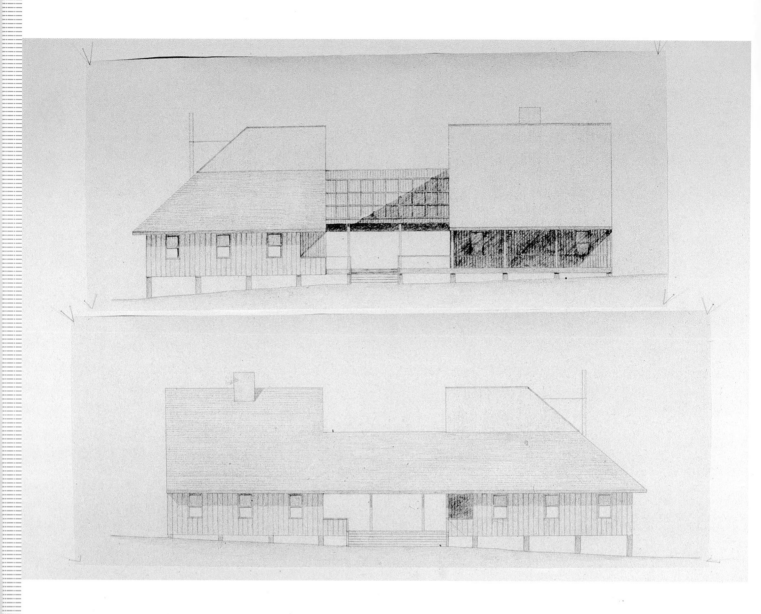

previous spread: Interior
view of the Cohen Memorial
Lodge at Camp Sequassen.
above: Elevation
renderings.
left: Construction view.
opposite: Detail of the barn
door.

above: Exterior view.

opposite: Entrance detail.

The client for the 1981 building project was Yale University, which needed an open-air pavilion for the Outdoor Education Center it maintains approximately forty-five miles east of New Haven in East Lyme, where lakeside cabins are offered for summer rental to students, faculty, alumni, and others affiliated with the university. Groups often rent several of the cabins and a large, sheltered pavilion was needed for these groups to prepare and eat their meals together. Formerly a campsite for the Yale Engineering Department, the 1,500 densely wooded acres were transformed into an Outdoor Education Center largely through the efforts of Edward Migdalski, an ichthyologist at the Bingham Oceanographic Laboratory, who was also instrumental in securing the commission for the architecture students. Named after its donor, Don Hopkins, an outdoorsman and member of the Yale College class of 1921, the wood pavilion stands at the base of a hill on the shore of Powers Lake.

The design divides the program into two components: a nine-hundred-square-foot eating hall connected by a covered walkway to a smaller pavilion equipped with a grill and serving area. Both volumes have tall gables with steep, twelve-in-twelve slopes. The smaller pavilion is set at a slight skew to the large one. The main volume has a plan that measures twenty-five by thirty-six feet; three bays formed by wood piers divide the long dimension. Generously sized picnic tables with benches are built into these bays.

The expression of structure is essential to the design. Each of the supporting piers is composed of six two-by-ten-inch Douglas Fir members bolted together and standing approximately twelve and a half feet tall, tied into wood lintels formed of four two-by-ten-inch members. A recessed metal blade embedded in the concrete foundation at the base of each of the built-up posts creates a minimal and elegant transition to the concrete floor. Steel cables in tension, instead of intermediate posts, are used to stabilize the structure to avoid interrupting the twenty-five-foot span of the main hall. The gable roof sits on a series of simple wood trusses that encircle the perimeter of the structure, creating, in effect, a clerestory level. Horizontal wood louvers at either end of the gable allow light to filter into the expansive interior volume.

The simple, almost primitive, forms of the Hopkins Pavilion suggest memories of refectories and rustic architecture appropriate to the building's function and setting.
— RWH

location: East Lyme, Connecticut

client: Yale University

project: Hopkins Pavilion at the Yale Outdoor Education Center

previous spread: The
Hopkins Pavilion at the Yale
Outdoor Education Center.
above: Construction
view with Toby Engelberg
and visitor.
opposite: Construction
views.

above: Roof detail.
opposite: The completed
building.

The 1982 project was for a pavilion and changing rooms in the town of Madison, Connecticut, located about twenty-five miles east of New Haven on the Long Island Sound. The design is composed of two elements — a wood gazebo on the beach, and combined changing rooms and toilet facilities located in a separate structure near the existing parking lot.

The pavilion, intended to provide shelter from the sun and wind on the portion of the shore called East Wharf Beach, is oriented to frame views of the Sound to the south and of Hammonassett Point to the east. The students designed a symmetrical, open-air wood gazebo standing on a thirty-foot-square concrete foundation. A mason instructed the students in sheathing the faces of the concrete base in Stony Creek granite, a local stone. For all visible parts of the gazebo, students used native Connecticut red oak, which was donated by a local lumber mill. In order to avoid having any interior columns, the students designed eight scissor trusses to support the pyramidal roof. These trusses meet at the base of a rooftop cupola and are held in place by metal ties in order to create a clear opening below the cupola. Measuring approximately eight feet square in plan, the cupola was constructed on site and then hoisted into place by a crane. The roof is sheathed in asphalt shingles.

The plan of the gazebo is composed of concentric layers of space that surround the central volume, which is about sixteen feet square and is open to the sky at its center. This central volume is defined by L-shaped partitions of wood lattice that hold wood benches. Above and on the interior side of each of the four wide openings are angled, horizontal bands of wood that add to the spatial complexity of the interior. The floor is composed of Douglas Fir in a concentric pattern. Since the pavilion was located in an environmentally sensitive area, the walkways that connect it to the parking lot and the changing rooms were fabricated out of duckboards that can be taken up during the off-season. Students also built a low skirt wall out of granite that connects the gazebo to the rock-faced East Wharf.

The combined changing rooms and toilet facilities are located in a compact, 170-square-foot structure faced with clapboard. A large exterior-mounted barn door serves to close off access to the changing rooms when the beach is closed.

The gazebo still serves its original function, although the original roof was replaced after a hurricane, and all of the wood has since been painted gray. Design team member David Scheer recalls that the pavilion served as a good place to watch the 1982 eclipse of the moon soon after the project was finished.
— RWH

location: Madison, Connecticut
client: The Town of Madison

project: Beach Pavilion and Changing Rooms

SECTION ELEVATION

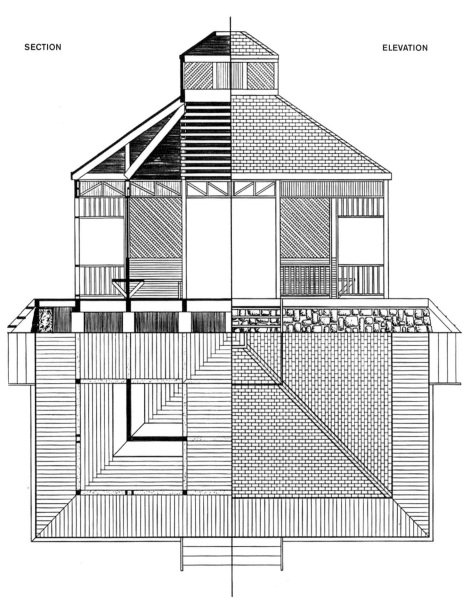

FLOOR PLAN ROOF PLAN

previous spread: Students
digging and setting out the
foundation.
above: Presentation drawing
of the selected design.
opposite: David Scheer.

opposite and above:
Interior and exterior views
of the completed building.

The 1983 building project was a concert stage on the New Haven Green, commissioned by the New Haven Department of Parks, Recreation and Trees. The City wanted to hold summer concerts for audiences numbering up to 25,000 people, and selected a site for the new stage in the eastern half of the park just south of Elm Street. The site is on axis with the memorial flagpole and fountain commemorating New Haven residents who died in the First World War.

A local civic organization, the Proprietors of the Common and Undivided Lands of the City of New Haven, exercises jurisdiction over the sixteen-acre, 370-year-old Green. The group maintained that the stage should be a temporary structure, so as not to compete with the three historic churches on the Green's west side. Consequently, an important component of the students' task was to design a structure that could be easily erected and then disassembled every year by the Parks Department employees.

The selected design was by a team of five women: Barbara Ball, Alison Friedman, Alison Noto, Marjorie Rothberg, and Christine Theodoropoulos, who had studied civil engineering at Princeton and was a licensed engineer before matriculating at Yale. Based on Ball's initial concept, their design was a simple, direct response to the program: a steel cube measuring forty feet on each side, containing a wood stage and supporting a canvas roof and a network of trusses from which to hang theatrical lights and speakers. The square plan evokes the nine-square grid of the original New Haven town plan. Working with Herman Spiegel, professor of structural engineering, Theodoropoulos assumed the lead in designing the structure for the project, and sought to simplify further the component elements, as well as minimize the number of connections.

The cube is made of eight-inch-square steel tubes bolted together to form the twelve members of the frame. Threaded rods serve as bracing. The stage is composed of a prefabricated wood deck supported on wood trusses. Twenty feet above the stage, the steel trusses are arranged in a grid of nine squares. Within the open volume above the trusses, a pyramid-shaped, prefabricated canvas tent is held in place by cables in tension. Following a suggestion by Paul Brouard, an enthusiastic sailor, the students used marine equipment to connect the tent to the cables.

The team arranged for as much of the construction as possible to occur off-site. Park City Steel, located in Orange, fabricated the steel tubes and provided the component elements for the trusses, which the students assembled in Hammond Hall, a cavernous building used by Yale's sculpture department. A professional welder, Susan Farricielli, instructed class members in tack welding, but was responsible for the structural welds. With most of the work completed off-site, assembly on the Green took only two weeks. A summer team led by Charles Loomis and Joseph Pasquinelli worked most days from mid-morning until late at night (discovering that work proceeded most quickly after dark). The steel tubes were originally painted red, the trusses painted black, and the canvas tent was white. Rectangular plywood panels painted blue served as backdrops for the stage. The Parks Department later painted all of these elements green.

After being demounted and reinstalled for almost twenty years, the stage is now a conditionally permanent fixture on the Green, serving as the setting for open-air concerts and theatrical performances that attract audiences to downtown New Haven.
— RWH

location: New Haven, Connecticut
client: The City of New Haven

project: Concert Stage on the Green

previous spread: Concert
stage on the New Haven
Green.
top: Kent Bloomer and
students.
bottom: Kristin Hawkins.
opposite: Plan, section,
and details of the stage.

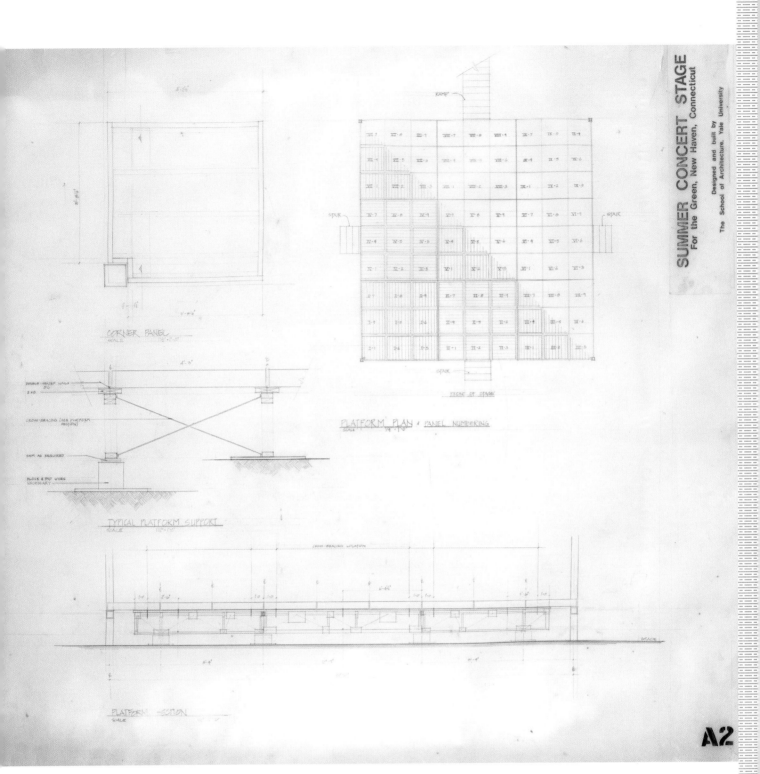

CORNER PANEL

TYPICAL PLATFORM SUPPORT

PLATFORM PLAN & PANEL NUMBERING

FRONT OF STAGE

PLATFORM SECTION

SUMMER CONCERT STAGE
For the Green, New Haven, Connecticut

Designed and built by
The School of Architecture, Yale University

A2

opposite and above:
Construction views.

The 1984 project, sponsored by the New Haven Department of Parks, Recreation and Trees, was a picnic pavilion in Lighthouse Point Park, an eighty-two-acre park located southeast of New Haven on a point that juts out into Long Island Sound. The combined wood, concrete, and metal pavilion is located on a knoll oriented towards the channel lighthouse on the breakwater that protects the New Haven Harbor from the Sound. Measuring roughly fifty feet by twenty feet, the 1,000-square-foot pavilion sits on a concrete base. A low masonry retaining wall built by the students from salvaged pieces of slate creates a three-sided perimeter at the rear of the structure. A secondary program requirement from the client was to provide a stage for performances, so the raised pavilion faces an open grass meadow suitable for gatherings.

The pavilion is composed of four open bays defined by two parallel rows of vertical piers that support a concavely curving roof. Each bay accommodates two picnic benches. According to design team member David Hotson, the design arose from a desire to make a vivid and dramatic statement using conventional materials. Designing during the heyday of stylistic postmodernism, the students were determined to avoid historical reference and nostalgic imagery. Instead, they emphasized the expression of structure. Each of the five tall piers on the land-facing side is assembled from thirteen pieces of two-by-eight-inch Douglas Fir lumber. Copper caps sheath the ends of the vertical members of these piers, the component pieces of which are tied together by redwood disks and threaded metal rods. For the opposing or harbor-facing piers, the students changed materials from wood to concrete. The five poured-in-place concrete supports take the form of halved, truncated cones. Atop each of the concrete piers, custom-fabricated metal connections receive the roof structure. The roof is supported by five splayed trusses made of Douglas Fir lumber. The truss members increase from two-by-six to two-by-twelve inches in depth as they fan out from the wood piers, increasing in length and ultimately cantilevering, finger-like, beyond the concrete piers at the opposite side. Much of the dramatic impact of the design results from the contrast between the planar wood piers and the curving profile of the roof.

Constructing the project during the summer months was an enjoyable experience for the class. Madeline Schwartzman remembers "regular crew dips in Long Island Sound, picnic lunches, and a relaxed summer atmosphere, in spite of the hard labor." Students built the entire pavilion, with the exception of the finished roofing and the custom metal connections where the roof trusses meet the concrete columns (one feature of which derives from the diagonal cut of the formwork, yielding a conical profile that suggests a modern interpretation of classical entasis). The pavilion is still in use, and park rangers refer to it affectionately as "the pagoda."
— RWH

project: Picnic Pavilion in Lighthouse Point Park

location: New Haven, Connecticut
client: The City of New Haven

previous spread: The picnic
pavilion in Lighthouse
Point Park.
above: Study model of one
of the roof trusses.
opposite: Final design
review.

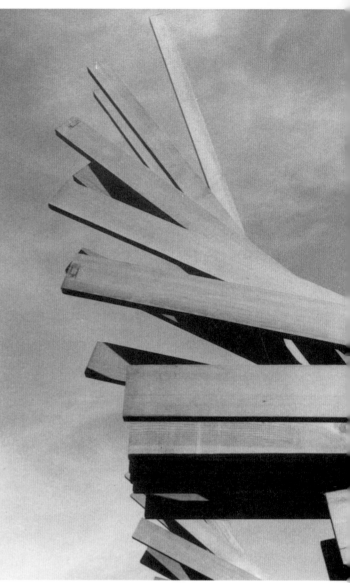

above and opposite:
Details and view of the
completed building.

As in the previous year, the program for the 1985 building project was a park pavilion, this time in East Rock Park in New Haven, in an area called College Woods at the terminus of Orange Street and opposite Wilbur Cross High School.

Placed on axis with a playground just to the west, the wood structure serves as an entrance pavilion to the Trowbridge Environmental Center, an educational facility maintained by the New Haven Department of Parks, Recreation and Trees. The pavilion, with its built-in tables and benches, provides a gathering and eating place for school groups visiting the Center.

Constructed of unpainted Douglas Fir, the pavilion has a biaxially symmetrical plan, measuring approximately thirty-two by forty feet. The main design gesture is a commodious roof formed of a wide gable extending along the east-west axis. The large scale of the gable responds to the pavilion's location, looking out over the Mill River and facing the abrupt three-hundred-foot rise of East Rock to the immediate north.

The plan is composed of seven rectangular bays organized about a central nave-like volume formed from the cross-axial plan. These bays are defined by piers constructed from clusters of six-by-six-inch wood posts. Four posts compose each pier; the wood members rest on square concrete plinths, fourteen inches tall. The four faces of each plinth are inscribed with decorative designs, such as leaves, fossils, and in one case, a miniature pictogram of the pavilion itself. Two generously proportioned wood tables with built-in benches are located on the north side of the pavilion. They now have almost twenty years' worth of names incised into their surfaces.

Students built the entire pavilion during the spring of 1985. Later that year, the design received an Elm-Ivy Award from Yale University, an award that recognizes achievements in improving the relationship between the university and New Haven. Since its construction, the only change to the pavilion has been a replacement of the roofing.
— RWH

location: New Haven, Connecticut
client: The City of New Haven

project: Pavilion at East Rock Park

previous spread: The
pavilion at East Rock Park.
above: Construction view.
left: Model of the selected
design.
opposite: Exterior view of
the completed building.

The client for the 1986 building project was Fort Nathan Hale Restoration Projects, Inc., a private, non-profit organization that supports the restoration of the Fort Nathan Hale historic site. The Civil War-era fort stands within a twenty-acre city park alongside New Haven Harbor on a site listed in the National Register of Historic Places. The organization needed a pavilion for the educational programs it offers to school groups and other visitors to the park. It would later be used as a setting for memorial services as well.

Located near the parking area among the dense marshes that characterize this part of the shoreline, the pavilion frames a view to the harbor in the near distance and provides a gathering place before visitors enter the historic sections of the park. The pavilion's design is strikingly modern. The major statement is a thin, curving roof in the shape of a radial arch. Sheathed in Douglas Fir on its underside, the concave shell of the roof is supported by two curved steel beams that stand on columns concealed inside concrete pylons. Park City Steel, which had fabricated the steel structure for the 1983 concert stage project, formed the curved beams in their workshop outside of New Haven. The angled concrete supports are assembled from prefabricated concrete panels that were lifted into place with a crane. Students looked for inspiration to the battered bunkers of the nineteenth-century fort when designing these sloping pylons. Extending between them, a gridded wood platform measures approximately twenty-eight by thirty-six feet. To the east, raised sections of the wood floor function as viewing platforms and provide space for moveable chairs when needed.

A wall composed of hemlock planks from recycled barn siding defines the south perimeter of the central space. Extending out into the landscape, it serves to conceal an unsightly view of the neighboring garage for the Marine Corps Reserve Unit. Articulated as a freestanding linear element, the wood wall also contains and conceals storage for park equipment. In front of it are built-in wood benches.

The design exploits the use of tactile surfaces in a limited, yet strong, palette of materials. The smooth, finished surfaces of the concrete pylons contrast with the adjacent rough-hewn, wide hemlock planks, similar to the way in which the curved steel beams stand out against the wood on the underside of the roof. The horizontal metal railings at the viewing platform are supported by minimal wood posts. At its easternmost end, the hemlock wall opens up to frame a columnar sculpture in welded steel designed and fabricated by student Bruce Graham.

The pavilion is at once inward-focused, offering a sheltered site for repose and reflection, and outward-facing, framing views of the historic landscape.
— RWH

location: New Haven, Connecticut
client: Fort Nathan Hale Restoration Projects, Inc.

project: Education Pavilion at Fort Nathan Hale

previous spread: The
education pavilion at Fort
Nathan Hale.
above: Aubrey Carter and
Andrew Berman.
left: Design sketch by
Aubrey Carter.
opposite: Exterior view.

above: Detail of the roof.
opposite: The pavilion in the landscape.

Bridgeport's Seaside Park is the site of the 1987 building project. Bordered by Cedar Creek and Black Rock Harbor to the northwest and the Long Island Sound to the south, this park was founded in the 1860s by Bridgeport's mayor, P.T. Barnum, the theatrical impresario, who hired Frederick Law Olmsted and Calvert Vaux as landscape architects. One hundred and twenty years later, the Bridgeport Parks Department found the waterfront park an ideal place to hold summer concerts. Acting as co-sponsors of the project, the City of Bridgeport and a local bank, Citytrust Bank, requested a stage of approximately 1,500 square feet for the Bridgeport Symphony. While the design phase was underway, the city altered the scope of the project as a result of successful negotiations with the New York City Philharmonic Orchestra, which agreed to play a series of Independence Day concerts at the new structure, requiring a stage of 2,500 square feet.

At the completion of the design phase, the clients selected a complex project inspired by the structure of a lobster shell. Students faced a setback in the construction schedule, however, due to an accident at the L'Ambience Plaza construction site in downtown Bridgeport in which twenty-eight workers died. The city's Building Department closed to investigate the incident, holding up the project's building permit for a month. The anticipated May 1–July 1 construction did not begin until June. Many students were unable to remain for the extended construction phase. The City subsequently promised to pay a group of twelve students to work throughout the summer, while Citytrust Bank covered the cost of materials. Thus, one of the most complex projects in the history of the program was completed by the one of the smallest groups of students in the Building Project's history.

According to class member Darin Cook, the construction crew encountered yet another difficulty once they were on-site. With a water table only eighteen inches below grade, water had to be pumped out of the ground while the foundations were dug, formed, and poured. Above the foundations, canted concrete piers were formed at an angle to receive the sloped base of the trusses. With each truss a unique dimension, each set of foundations required separate formwork. The six trusses needed to realize the shell were manufactured in two segments off-site, then connected by plywood gusset plates and raised into position by a crane. The largest truss is thirty-six feet tall and fifty-five feet wide. The precision of the manufactured trusses required exact placement of the foundations and angle of the finished face and bearing plate. Due to the late start and delayed foundation work, the crew was unable to finish the project by the end of summer, causing the bank to hire a construction company to sheath the structure, and the City to pledge to pay the class for an additional eight to ten weeks of labor the following summer.

Over the winter, the class developed a system for roofing the complex form with 9,000 square feet of uniform, sixteen-inch-square copper shingles. Folded on all edges — the lower sides folded under, the upper folded over — the shingles locked together at the folds, slightly offset from each other. The geometry of the roof was divided into thirty-six flat facets designed to bridge the six trusses of the underlying structure. Beginning in May 1988, each facet was preassembled on-site with the interlocking copper shingles. As each facet was attached to the structure, flat-seam flashing was applied around the upper edge and sides of each panel. The next layer of facets was then attached at an angle, so that water would shed over the seam to the facet below. The final step in readying the structure for performance was completed as the inner shell of acoustically engineered panels were delivered and attached to the underside of the trusses.

Although opening a year later than initially planned, the stage proved successful as a concert venue, hosting the New York Philharmonic at Fourth of July concerts for many years.
— MB

location: Bridgeport, Connecticut
client: The City of Bridgeport and Citytrust Bank

project: Concert Pavilion

previous spread: The
concert pavilion in
Bridgeport, Connecticut.
above and opposite:
Construction views.

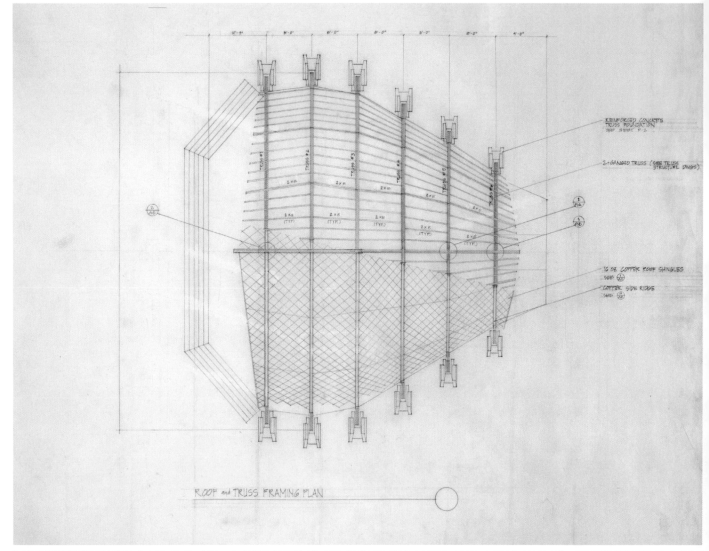

ROOF and TRUSS FRAMING PLAN

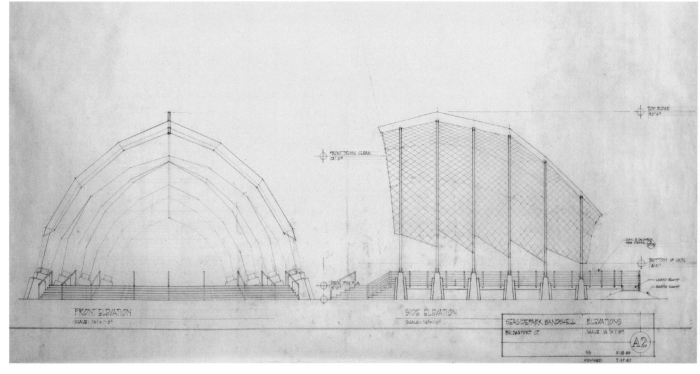

FRONT ELEVATION

SIDE ELEVATION

SEASIDE PARK BANDSHELL   ELEVATIONS
BRIDGEPORT CT.

A2

opposite top: Roof and truss
framing plan.
opposite bottom: Elevations.
above: Exterior view of the
completed building.

In 1988, the town of East Lyme, Connecticut, issued a request for proposals for a new meeting hall, to be built on a historic farm on the site of a demolished barn that once stood adjacent to the landmark Smith-Harris House. Built circa 1845 for Thomas Avery and listed on the National Register of Historic Places, the Smith-Harris House was transformed into the East Lyme Town Museum during the 1976 national Bicentennial Celebration. The client wanted a large enclosed space that could accommodate a variety of events, such as demonstrating sheep shearing or reading ghost stories to children on Halloween.

According to class member Roberto Espejo, students were initially surprised by what seemed like the modest nature of the project, but gradually warmed up to the challenge after visiting the site and meeting the clients, to whom they presented a great variety of schemes at the initial review: "There were tall barns, fat barns, long barns. There were barns lifted right out of history books, as well as modern ones that seemed to have been twisted by the wind. There were barns with slits in the walls mimicking old barns for drying tobacco."

The winning design reinterpreted the original nineteenth-century barn in an elegant, straightforward fashion, incorporating post and beam construction. The remains of the original stone foundation determined the hall's overall thirty-by-fifty-foot dimension. The students designed a 1,500-square-foot, gable-roofed volume divided into five bays by six king post trusses, each consisting of a bottom chord, central post, and two heavy diagonal arms supported by smaller diagonals. Exposed timber knee bracing structurally reinforces the trusses and visually enlivens the interior.

After pouring a new concrete foundation, the students erected and stabilized the trusses, then marked the completion with a celebration (see essay by Hayes, pp. 38–39). The meeting hall's minimal exteriors were sheathed in unpainted tongue-in-groove cedar siding (since painted red) with cedar shingles covering the roof.

The placement of the door and window openings continued the theme of a modern interpretation of the original barn. Large barn doors mounted on exterior tracks were located on the south, east, and west elevations. On the north — the side facing the woods — sliding doors were designed to open up almost the entire elevation, treating the surrounding nature as decorative "wallpaper" when viewed from the interior, according to Espejo. Rectangular glazed openings above the barn doors on the two end elevations mimic traditional haylofts.

Class member Matt Bucy recorded the construction in a short film, which had its premiere in the barn at the communal barbecue celebrating the project's completion.
— MB

location: Village of Niantic, Connecticut
client: Town of East Lyme

project: Meeting Hall, Smith-Harris Farm

previous spread: Interior
view of the meeting hall in
East Lyme, Connecticut.
opposite and above: Interior
and exterior views.

1989 marked a turning point in the history of the Yale Building Project: students designed and built a two-family house for the New Haven chapter of Habitat for Humanity, and in so doing inaugurated a commitment to affordable housing in New Haven that has lasted for eighteen years. Kari Nordstrom, an alumnus of the School of Architecture and a board member of Habitat, suggested the idea of working with the Georgia-based non-profit organization to Paul Brouard and Herbert Newman, who agreed to a departure from the pavilions and recreation structures that had been the focus of the Building Project for most of the 1970s and '80s.

The site was an abandoned lot, fifty feet wide by one-hundred feet deep, on Hallock Street in the Hill, one of the poorest neighborhoods in New Haven. Named for Gerard Hallock, a nineteenth-century developer of this quarter, which was also known as the Third Ward, Hallock Street is characterized by a mixture of housing types: compact wood-frame houses with frontal gables; two-family "double-deckers" with street-facing porches; and a few masonry apartment buildings, in addition to one small mansard-roofed, octagonal house, described by architectural historian Elizabeth Mills Brown as "an architectural oddity" (Elizabeth Mills Brown, *New Haven: A Guide to Architecture and Urban Design* (New Haven: Yale University Press, 1976)).

According to class member Michael Wetstone, student discussion during the design phase focused on how contextual the new building should be, and whether the two houses should be placed back-to-back, one atop the other, or side-by-side. The selected design, by a team originally composed of John Gilmer, Diana Greenberg, Susan Sutton, and Claire Theobald, placed the two houses adjacent to one another in a single volume, approximately thirty-two feet wide and fifty-four feet deep. Each house holds a living room, dining room, kitchen, and powder room on the ground floor; three bedrooms and a bathroom on the second floor; and a full basement and attic. Opening off the kitchens are small nooks that offer space for eating and for observing the back yards.

The façade on Hallock Street is composed of two intersecting gables that identify the units as distinct residences. Claire Theobald notes that the design idea was to give each of the homes its own identity, suggesting two separate houses. The students used a number of devices, besides the twin gables, to differentiate them. The southernmost house, painted blue, has a wide front porch with its long dimension parallel to the street. The adjacent house, painted light gray, has a narrow porch that opens onto the side yard, rather than the street. A gable on the side elevation of this house reinforces its connection to the side yard, and looks out across a few open lots toward Congress Avenue.

After the entire class worked on-site during the spring semester, a team of four students stayed on through the summer to continue construction, joined periodically by volunteers from Habitat for Humanity and the future homeowners. Alisa Dworsky remembers the public quality of life on Hallock Street that summer — so different from the empty blocks in the Orange Street neighborhood that she returned home to each evening. For another team member, Diana Greenberg, "the sheer, rewarding physicality of the construction work" was matched by the chance "to see upfront how buildings get made: pouring concrete on a rainy day; operating a jackhammer; lifting up pre-framed walls; nailing black shingles onto the roof on a hot day in August." Habitat completed the interior finishes during the fall of 1989.

One of the two original families still resides in their house.
— RWH

location: New Haven, Connecticut
client: Habitat for Humanity of Greater New Haven

project: Two-Family House at 63–65 Hallock Street

previous spread: The
two-family house under
construction.
above: Construction views.
opposite: Street façade of
the completed building.

The 1990 building project was the second residence and the second partnership with Habitat for Humanity. As in 1989, the project was a two-family house, and the winning scheme proposed two separate houses linked by a small connecting volume. Unfortunately, due to legal and regulatory difficulties that led to problems selling the houses, one of the houses fell into disrepair and was eventually demolished.

Rosette Street is in the Hill neighborhood of New Haven, which, in its heyday around 1920 was one of the City's largest and most diverse urban communities, filled with apartment buildings, houses, corner shops, churches, and schools. As with much of working-class New Haven, the neighborhood fell prey to changing demographics and urban renewal. A major factor was the construction of the Oak Street Connector (Route 34), a wide, sunken freeway built in the early 1960s, which severed the neighborhood from downtown. Today, The Hill is isolated, surrounded by the Metro-North rail lines and Route 95 to the south, the metastasizing Yale-New Haven Hospital to the north, and marshy wetlands to the west. Rosette Street is quiet and poor, with many vacant lots and run-down houses.

The site for the 1990 building project was a narrow, thirty-five-foot-wide lot. Required setbacks and space for a driveway reduced the buildable area, and limited the students' options for arranging two residences on the lot. Two of the three finalists proposed long, single buildings with apartments separated by interior party walls. The winning scheme proposed two separate houses, each with its own architectural identity, connected only minimally at their backdoors. The front house, which still exists, maintains the street wall and mimics the massing and front porches of its neighbors, intended to evoke the working-class houses on the block that date from the early years of the twentieth century.

Although the back house had the same footprint as the front one, it was different in almost every other regard. Pushed well into the back yard, it became part of the block's interior — a large, open area formed by neighboring back yards. To accentuate the relationship of the house to this open volume, the gable roof was turned perpendicular to that of the front house, running along the short axis of the plan and resulting in a dramatically different massing. The large façade of the rear house looked down the long interior of the block, taking possession of the open space. The entry was centered on this façade, and the door's scale was inflated by a decorative surround. Large, traditionally expressed corner boards added to the house's presence, so that it read as a vestigial manor house whose estate had been subdivided and absorbed into the growing urban grid.

These subtle moves — proposing two independent structures and expressing the two houses differently, which led to the back house having a strong identity — won the commission. Unfortunately, one of the motivations for giving the back house presence and visibility (namely, safety, in a neighborhood where places hidden from public view lead to trouble) was part of what led to its demise. The two houses were seen by the City as a multi-unit condominium, and as such, a higher degree of culpability was demanded from the developers — ostensibly Yale University and Habitat for Humanity. This issue had arisen during the previous project, and to resolve things the University wrote a letter assuming some responsibility for construction that year. They would not do so again, however, and the project entered a state of legal limbo. Although Habitat builds its houses only after they have found a buyer (the future residents often work on the construction of their houses), in this case they never completed the transaction. Habitat thus maintained ownership and made the two houses rental properties. A string of transient residents ensued. The back house, despite the students' good intentions, became a magnet for crime and neglect and after several years was torn down.
— TW

location: New Haven, Connecticut
client: Habitat for Humanity of Greater New Haven

project: Two-Family House at 133 Rosette Street

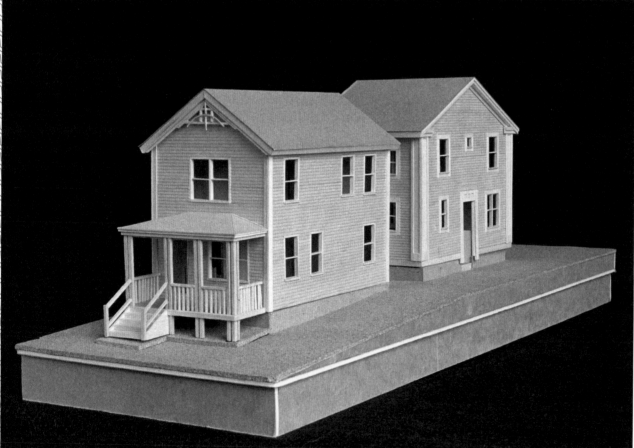

previous spread: The street
façade during construction.
opposite: Model of the
selected design.
above: Exterior views of the
completed building.

In 1991, students designed and built a two-family house for a New Haven-based non-profit organization called Home, Inc. Founded in 1987, Home, Inc. builds and manages rental housing for low-income families in Greater New Haven. Located on Blake Street in the Westville neighborhood, the houses stand in the southeast corner of a rectangular three-quarter-acre lot adjacent to the Mishkan Israel Cemetery. Temple Mishkan Israel, a reform congregation in Hamden originally founded in New Haven, owns the land, which it is leasing for a nominal fee to Home, Inc. for a period of fifty years. Funding for the project came from a number of sources, including the Greater New Haven Community Loan Fund.

A variety of housing types characterizes the neighborhood: nineteenth-century Greek Revival houses with frontal gables that are close to the street; early-twentieth-century, porch-fronted houses with deep front yards; and more recent apartment buildings in a modern vocabulary. Composed of two houses with separate entrances and sharing a party wall, the students' design reflects these neighborhood types. The southernmost house is close to and parallel with the street and has a frontal gable similar to the existing wood-frame house next door. The second house is set back from the street at a slight angle to the first house, and has a long porch that wraps around the façade and part of the side elevation. Design team member Gitta Robinson notes that the intention was to suggest separate identities for each of the rental units, so the porches and windows were placed so as to minimize views from one house into the other. The location of the skewed house serves to conceal a parking area in the rear. Part of the students' design scope included planning the entire site, where Home, Inc. intended to install six other prefabricated rental units and build a common parking area.

Each house has a ground floor containing a living room, dining area, kitchen, and powder room, and a second floor with three bedrooms and a bathroom. Where the houses meet is articulated as a service zone holding the stairs, bathrooms, and powder rooms. Recessed slightly from the adjacent volumes, this service core has large windows on the street façade that bring daylight into the two back-to-back staircases. The modern style of these windows contrasts with the historical character of the overall design.

Clapboard painted light gray and double-hung stock windows characterize the exterior of both houses. The wood railings on the two porches have a mixture of horizontal and vertical members. Interior finishes include white-painted walls, periwinkle blue tiles in the bathrooms and kitchens, and wood railings for the staircases. After the completion of the two-family house, Home, Inc. installed the six other rental units, which have noticeably less character and detail than the double house designed by the class of 1993.
— RWH

project: Two-Family House on Blake Street

location: New Haven, Connecticut
client: Home, Inc. of New Haven

project: Two-Family House on Blake Street

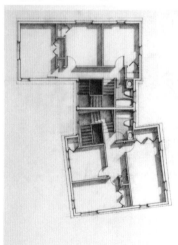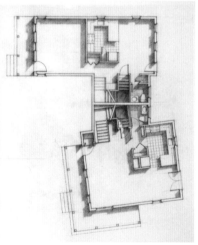

previous spread: Street
façade.
top: Standing from left:
Erica Moon, Chris Arelt,
Gitta Robinson, Alexandra
Iselin, George Clemens,
Evan Supcoff. Seated from
left: Nora Demeter, Jordan
Levin, Bettina Stark.
bottom: Rendered plans.

above: Scott Specht and
classmates.

opposite: Greg Barnell.
above top: Charles Lazor.
above bottom: Students
at work.

Exterior view of the
completed houses.

Located on Newhall Street, the 1992 building project embodies a synthesis of two discernible architectural ideas: on the one hand, the design of the house can be understood as contextual — with a street-facing porch, a frontal gable articulated with applied ornament, and clapboard siding that relate to the neighboring houses. On the other hand, the house has a unique character independent of its specific setting that is articulate and self-referential.

Newhall Street runs roughly parallel to Dixwell Avenue in the Newhallville neighborhood, home to New Haven's oldest and largest African-American community. The neighborhood occupies the area just north of Yale's Payne Whitney Gymnasium, stretching about a mile to the town border with Hamden. Newhallville was once the unofficial company town for Winchester Repeating Arms which at its peak between the World Wars employed almost 21,000 New Haven residents. By mid-century, however, the neighborhood was immersed in social change: a mass migration of poor African-Americans to northern cities in search of manufacturing jobs swelled Newhallville, as new technologies and cheap labor made it profitable to move factories outside of cities and, eventually, out of the country. By the late 1960s, the area was stunted by unemployment and convulsed by unrest, and by the 1980s some of its blocks were the most murderous in the nation — a situation worsened by the crack cocaine epidemic.

During the months in which the class of 1994 worked on the house, *The New Yorker* published a series of articles (subsequently gathered together as a book by journalist William Finnegan) about a family in the Newhallville neighborhood caught up in a cycle of drug and alcohol addiction, poverty, and gang activity. A vacant lot described in the articles as a hub of the city's drug trade was about a half block from the site. The project, nevertheless, moved forward without any problems, and coincided with an effort by the New Haven police to combat crime in the neighborhood.

The front porch of the 1992 building project participates in the community formed by its neighboring porches, while introducing a theme unique to its design carried out throughout the first floor of the house. The students treated the porch railing as a datum organizing elements of the interior and exterior design. For example, on the interior, a half-height partition separating the living room from the entrance hall aligns with the top of the railing. On the exterior, vertically oriented siding forms a wainscot and aligns with the top of the railing; on the south side of the house, however, a two-story projecting bay containing the staircase interrupts it.

In response to the protruding bay, the first floor of the southwest corner of the house is opened up, creating a balance of positive and negative space in the overall massing. A generously sized rear porch extends into the back yard from this voided corner and serves as a weather shelter outside the kitchen. The rear porch — in contrast to the front porch which is covered by a shed roof — has a trabeated pergola, the grid of which is integrated into the volume of the house. Posts composed of rectangular members painted charcoal grey support both the rear pergola and the front shed roof. Students articulated the pergola as an open-air object that nestles into the solid form of the gabled volume, and serves as a transitional space between the house and the back yard.

From the back porch, a rear entrance leads to the kitchen and looks into the dining area, which is separated by another half-height partition that echoes the one dividing the living room from the entry. The partial enclosure conceals kitchen clutter and admits abundant daylight streaming from the dining area's south-facing casement windows into both rooms. A switchback stair and swing space separate this dual space from the living room in the front of the first floor.

Sectional variation occurs within the spacious double-height stairwell: a built-in seat for reading is located on an oversized landing and a multipurpose space is created a few steps above the top landing as a consequence of the higher ceiling in the dining area. Horizontally oriented clerestory windows illuminate the

location: New Haven, Connecticut
client: Habitat for Humanity of Greater New Haven

project: House at 316 Newhall Street

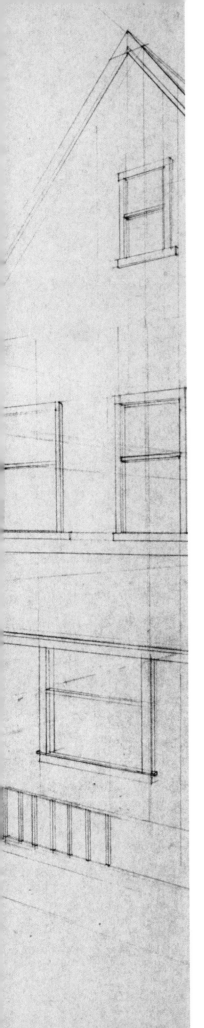

staircase and are matched by interior clerestory windows atop the second-floor partitions. The taut exterior is enlivened by a mixture of double-hung case-ment and awning windows. It was originally painted mint green with a band of dark grey beneath the eaves matching the exterior posts.

The urban and social issues related to this project encouraged one student, Regina L. Winters, to work for the City of New Haven after she graduated. For many years, she worked for the Livable City Initiative and served for a short time in 2005 as interim executive director of the City of New Haven Housing Authority.
— Tim Applebee (TA)

previous spread:
Street façade.
left: Perspective drawing.
above: Model.

EAST ELEVATION · NEWHALL STREET

top left and opposite:
Construction views.
bottom left: Working
drawing.

above: Construction view.
opposite: The completed
building from the rear.

The 1993 building project is a block away from the 1992 house on Newhall Street in New Haven and represents the fourth partnership with Habitat for Humanity. The first two were two-family houses, but in 1992 a switch was made to single-family projects with Habitat. The next three houses present very similar street façades: tall and narrow, gable-roofed.

Habitat asked that the house fit in with its surroundings and recommended using the 1992 house as a model. Pressure on students from clients and critics to produce designs using the architectural language of neighboring houses (i.e., to design "traditional"-looking houses) has ebbed and flowed throughout the years of the Building Project, as has student reaction. The parti of the 1993 house presents one of the more dramatic attempts to be concurrently traditional and modern. The front third is a gabled, clapboard volume with massing very similar to the 1992 house, while the back is a minimal, white, board-and-batten box with a shed roof rising to the back.

The students resisted tradition through unusual siting. First, the house is set back about twenty feet from its neighbors, breaking the street wall. Second, unlike its neighbors, which are oriented perpendicularly to Newhall Street, it is angled to align with Cave Street, which dead-ends at an angle into Newhall directly across from the site. Driving toward it on one-way Cave Street, one sees the 1993 house centered at the end.

The large setback is designed to push the house into the back yard, where it receives unobstructed southern sunlight. The siting helps generate the interior plan. An outdoor deck is placed at this house's mid-point on the south side, taking advantage of the sun exposure, and is pushed into the house's volume, creating a two-story negative space. This tall outdoor room separates the traditional front from the more modern back.

The living room is at the front of the first story, and the master bedroom at the front of the second. A porch is accessible from the living room, although not from the yard or street. Instead, the main entrance is on the north side at the mid-point of the house, and opens into a narrow hall that slips along the edge of the outdoor room. At the rear are the kitchen and dining areas and a stair. At the back of the second floor are two bedrooms and the master bedroom.

At the end of construction, a raucous opening party was held. It was attended by the mayor and the Yale Precision Marching Band, a noisy, comedic band that specializes in playing rock songs on wind instruments and marching in ragged, flamboyant formations. Some students were uncomfortable with the noisy show — especially after their months of careful outreach to neighbors, many of whom were suspicious of the Building Project's motives. Soon afterward, the house was vandalized. The situation in the largely African-American neighborhood was possibly exacerbated by the Hispanic background of the owners who, like the Yale student builders, were seen as outsiders.

Although Newhallville has become a safer, more vibrant neighborhood in recent years, in part due to the efforts of Habitat for Humanity and Neighborhood Housing Services, the blocks around the 1992 and 1993 houses remained dangerous for a few years following construction. The intersection of Newhall and Read was the focus of intensive anti-drug trafficking efforts, including surveillance by helicopters and a deployment of the National Guard. This period, one of New Haven's bleakest, passed. Today, both houses are occupied and well maintained.
— TW

location: New Haven, Connecticut
client: Habitat for Humanity of Greater New Haven
project: House at 348 Newhall Street

previous spread: Rear
façade.

left: Rendered section and
plans.

opposite: The design team
and their models. Top row
standing from left: Hugh
Patterson, Mike Levy, Seung
Park, Todd Stodolski, Dolly
Hernandez, David Taylor,
Lloyd Fisk, Eric Cheng.
Bottom row from left: Jamie
Unkefer, Katherine Ann Yi,
Russ Katz, Issa Diabate.

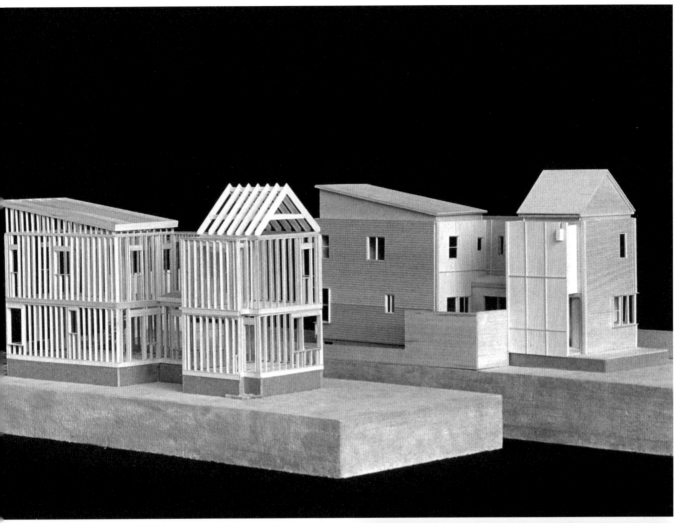

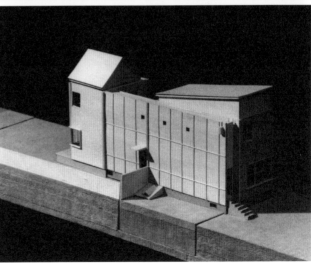

opposite: Construction views.
above: Students top from left:
Christine Clemons, Aaron
Lamport, Todd Stodolski,
Laura King, high school
intern, Eric Andreason, high
school intern. Bottom from
left: Andrew McCune and
George Knight.

left and opposite:
Exterior views of the
completed house.

The 1994 building project was another cooperative effort between the School of Architecture and Habitat for Humanity of Greater New Haven. Unfortunately, Dewitt Street in the Hill neighborhood was one of the most threatening social environments of any of the building projects, and a gang fight broke out during the summer the house was constructed.

The narrow street frontage of the site necessitated a thin, deep floor plan to accommodate the 1,500-square-foot program, featuring a gabled façade and roofed front porch running along the southern and eastern perimeter of the living room. The location of the front entrance, recessed from the street, constitutes a unique variation of neighboring porches, in which visitors can only enter the house after walking past the living room. While the living area monitors the front, the dining room overlooks the rear yard and sizeable deck. At the middle of the house, a staircase leads to three upstairs bedrooms, two at the back and one in front. A clerestory lights the stairwell.

Several design features respond to the solar orientation of the site. As the front porch wraps around the side of the house, it shades the living room from southern sun exposure and mitigates solar gain. The clerestory windows in the stairwell face south, brightening the middle section, which falls in the shade of the neighboring apartment building. Three southern-facing solar panels mounted on the roof provide a supplemental means of heating potable water, whereby anti-freeze circulates through pipes between the panels and hot water tank, transferring heat from one to the other. The panels were installed by Sun Search, Inc., a company operated by faculty member Everett Barber.

Michael Knopoff, a member of the design team, remembers the experience as both exhausting and "a lot of fun, due to the winning attitude of our unflappable crew leader...sipping his tea, making sure his classmates were working on their tasks."

The original homeowners have lived in the house for the past twelve years, where they have raised a family in a house they helped build.
— TA

location: New Haven, Connecticut
client: Habitat for Humanity of Greater New Haven

project: House at 92 Dewitt Street

previous spread:
Street façade.
top left: Model of the
selected design.
bottom left: Herb Newman.
above: Deborah Berke, Fred
Koetter, and students.

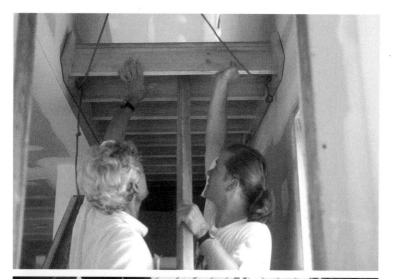

left top: Paul Brouard and
Michael Koch.
left bottom and above:
Construction views.

The three-bedroom, 1,250-square-foot house on Cassius Street in New Haven's Hill neighborhood is the last project for Habitat for Humanity, and the smallest house so far in the program's history. According to design team member Alexander Barrett, the students sited the rectangular, clapboard-sided house with its long dimension parallel to the street so that the compact design would not appear diminutive.

In the interior, a centrally placed staircase divides the house into public and private zones. To the left of the staircase, a large, rectangular living room spans the depth of the house. To the right of the stair, a passage leads from a small entrance hall past a powder room and coat closet to the kitchen and dining area. On the second floor, two small bedrooms are located above the living area, with a master bedroom above the entrance, powder room, and kitchen.

A shed-roofed, two-story volume forms a saddle-bag-like extension to the back of the house. On the ground floor, it holds a dining area open to the kitchen, both of which have slate tile flooring. On the second floor above the dining area, the extension contains a bathroom, located so as to maximize space for the bedrooms.

Acknowledging the limited square footage of the house, the students sought to design the exterior as an extension of the interior. Along the east side of the house, the living room cantilevers over a concrete wall, which forms part of the foundation and extends into the back yard as a linear element separating the driveway from a rear deck. At the front, this wall forms a terminus to a built-in planter. Toward the rear, the wall is punctured by stairs that lead to the back door. The deck at the back of the house creates an exterior living and dining space, with wide steps down to the deep back yard.

One of the requirements of Habitat for Humanity was that the students had to limit their choice of materials to siding and windows that had already been donated to the organization. Working within these parameters, the designers sought to use stock components in such a way as to suggest a custom design. For example, in the master bedroom, they grouped three small windows together to create one large opening. Also in the master bedroom, they suggested that two stock windows placed at the northwest corner were custom by trimming the opening in such a way that minimizes the corner post. To create a distinct façade on the yard side of the dining alcove, the students designed three framed openings that extend from floor to ceiling to hold large, double-hung windows. Built with a limited set of materials and comprising a tight square footage, the house is cleverly and efficiently designed — from the site to the interior arrangement of spaces. Although the house has been sold a few times since its completion, William Casey, the executive director of Habitat for Humanity of Greater New Haven, considers its design to be among the most successful of the six houses his organization and Yale have built together.
— MB

location: New Haven, Connecticut
client: Habitat for Humanity of Greater New Haven

project: House at 10 Cassius Street

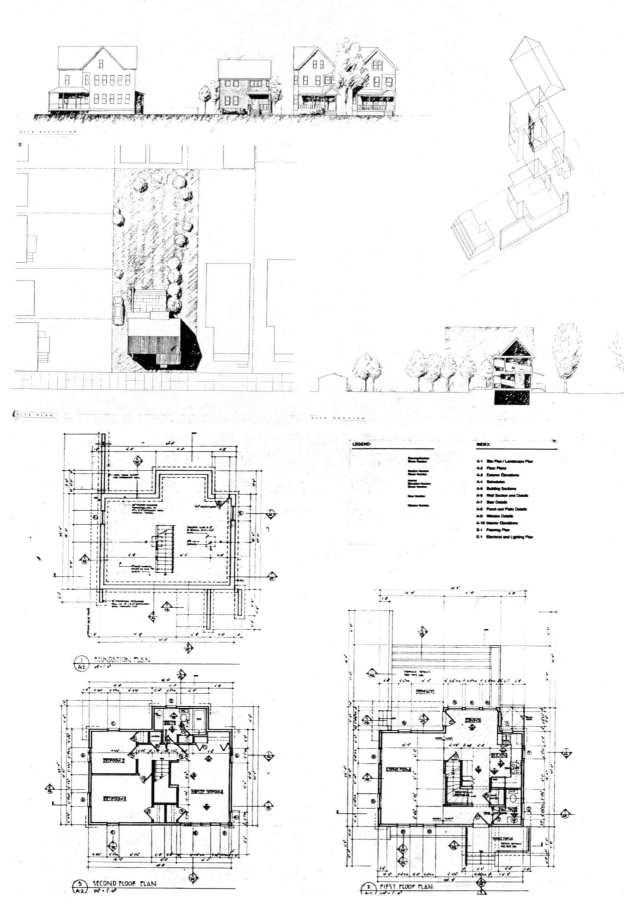

SITE ELEVATION

SITE PLAN

SITE SECTION

LEGEND:

INDEX:

A-1   Site Plan / Landscape Plan
A-2   Floor Plans
A-3   Exterior Elevations
A-4   Schedules
A-5   Building Sections
A-6   Wall Section and Details
A-7   Stair Details
A-8   Porch and Patio Details
A-9   Window Details
A-10 Interior Elevations
S-1   Framing Plan
E-1   Electrical and Lighting Plan

FOUNDATION PLAN

SECOND FLOOR PLAN

FIRST FLOOR PLAN

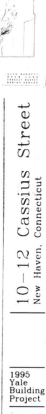

10—12 Cassius Street
New Haven, Connecticut

1995
Yale
Building
Project

FLOOR
PLANS

24 APRIL 1995
¼" = 1'0"

A-2

previous spread:
Street façade.
left top: Site elevation, plan, and section.
left bottom: Floor plans.
right top and bottom: Model of the selected design.
overleaf: Paul Brouard with William Greaves, Martina Choi, and Thomas Gluck.

The long-running partnership between the School of Architecture and Neighborhood Housing Services of New Haven began in 1996 with a single-family house at 136 Cedar Hill Avenue, located near East Rock Park. Built on two adjacent lots purchased from the City of New Haven, the project participates in a de-densification effort by the City to combine empty lots in order to spark neighborhood revitalization. Since the new house would have a program requiring only 1,500 square feet, the students faced the challenge of building in a context of much larger neighboring houses. The form of the selected design, two intersecting rectangular volumes, maximizes the street frontage while sheltering a more private back deck and yard. A switchback stair occupies the interstitial space where the two volumes intersect, creating distinct front and back zones inside the house.

The front door opens into the main living space from a twenty-three-foot-long porch. A powder room and closet are to the right of the entry, with the switchback stair beyond. Past the stair, the dining area abuts a U-shaped kitchen on one side, and on the other a deck that acts as an extension of the living area. The kitchen features a side door to the driveway. Hardwood flooring distinguishes the circulation space from the carpeted living area and the tiled kitchen floor. Occupying the rectangular slot of space between the front and rear volumes, the stair leads to a landing designed as an intermediate space between the public ground floor and the private second floor. It contains a low, built-in bench, providing additional living space, as well as extra storage.

On the second floor, the master bedroom and bathroom fill the back volume above the dining area and kitchen, while two smaller bedrooms share access to a second full bathroom in the front volume.

On the exterior, the two intersecting volumes are articulated by opposing shed roofs, both sheathed in asphalt shingles. The front volume slopes down to the south, while the shed roof at the back rises at a sharper angle. The rear shed roof peaks when it reaches the height of the front shed, from that point turning down to follow the line of the front volume. Painted horizontal cedar siding clads both volumes. At the back of the house, the south wall of the living room extends as a low planter alongside the deck, establishing a boundary between the deck and the neighboring house. The deck opens into the back yard with a wide stair.

The final element on the site, a carport, was completed by the students in the fall. This third volume is located to the north and west of the house at the end of the driveway. The only car shelter so far among the house projects, it was designed to complete the shed roof profile and to bridge the space between the new house and the larger neighboring house.
— MB

location: New Haven, Connecticut
client: Neighborhood Housing Services of New Haven

project: House at 136 Cedar Hill Avenue

1996

previous spread:
Exterior view.
opposite and above:
Construction views.

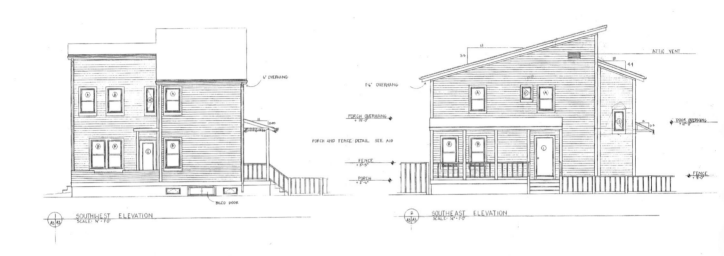

6' OVERHANG

1'-6' OVERHANG

PORCH OVERHANG
+15'-0"

PORCH AND FENCE DETAIL. SEE A10

ATTIC VENT

DOOR OVERHANG
+10'-0"

FENCE
+5'-5"

PORCH
+3'-0"

FENCE
+5'-0"

BILCO DOOR

SOUTHWEST ELEVATION
SCALE: ¼" = 1'-0"

SOUTHEAST ELEVATION
SCALE: ¼" = 1'-0"

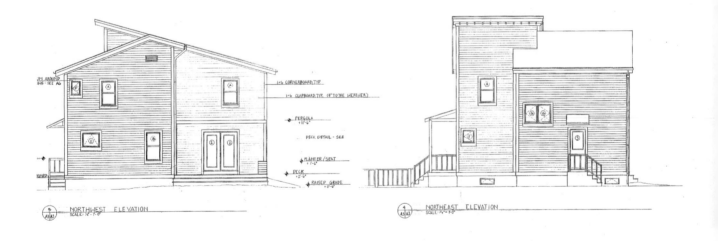

JM AROUND
AWB - SEE A6

1×6 CORNERBOARD, TYP.

1×6 CLAPBOARD, TYP. (4" TO THE WEATHER)

PERGOLA
+11'-6"

DECK DETAIL - SEE

PLANTER / SEAT
+1'-0"

DECK
+2'-6"

RAISED GRADE
+0'-0"

RAMP

NORTHWEST ELEVATION
SCALE: ¼" = 1'-0"

NORTHEAST ELEVATION
SCALE: ¼" = 1'-0"

opposite: Elevation
drawings.
above: Street façade.

The prominent site for the 1997 building project — at the corner of Derby Avenue and Winthrop Street in the West River neighborhood of New Haven — is cater-corner to a public square and across from a squat, neoclassical church. The square is formed at the point where Derby Avenue peels off of Chapel Street at an angle to the street grid, creating a series of triangular blocks and acute corners, of which the site is the first.

The houses on Derby Avenue address the street at an angle, conforming to the neighborhood grid. The houses on Winthrop have a traditional relationship to the street, their façades parallel to it. The winning design takes both conditions into account, placing the entrance on Derby at an angle, but folding acutely at the corner to maintain the street wall on Winthrop.

The site strategy ripples through the design at several scales tectonically and visually, using both color and texture. To call out the house's alignment to Winthrop Street, the façade is "broken" — stepped in eighteen inches — and the resulting gap glazed. The effect is to render the wall parallel to the street as a plane. This decision is reinforced by a change in color and cladding: the main wall is a pale yellow clapboard, and the boxy, angled volume at the back is a green board-and-batten. Approached from the south via Winthrop Street, the green volume's angle echoes the unusual angle of Derby Avenue and the orientation of the plan.

As with many Building Project houses, the students were challenged to address, and even match, the large scale of the neighboring houses with a scant 1,500-square-foot program. In this case, students stepped up the roofline toward the corner of the site in a neck-stretching attempt to match the eave heights along Derby Avenue, while gesturing towards church and square. One by-product is the creation of a double-height master bedroom with tall, triple-hung windows.

The site's required setbacks left a thin footprint, resulting in shallow interiors akin to the 'shotgun' plans common in the Deep South. A maple plywood-clad wall further divides the house along its long axis, and contains the service elements: storage, kitchen appliances, mechanical equipment, and plumbing. Stock cabinets were purchased and installed flush with the dividing wall; their doors were removed and replaced with maple to match the surrounding panels. A clerestory made of Lucite panels forms the top of the dividing wall on both stories, allowing natural light to fill the house throughout the day.

During construction, the students realized that the stair ascended directly toward the stepped-in section of roof and seized the opportunity to create a skylight. Expressed like an open trap door, it is emblematic of the house's overall architecture — a composition of planes operating both spatially and programmatically at once.
— Tarra Cotterman and TW

location: New Haven, Connecticut
client: Neighborhood Housing Services of New Haven

project: House at 50 Derby Avenue

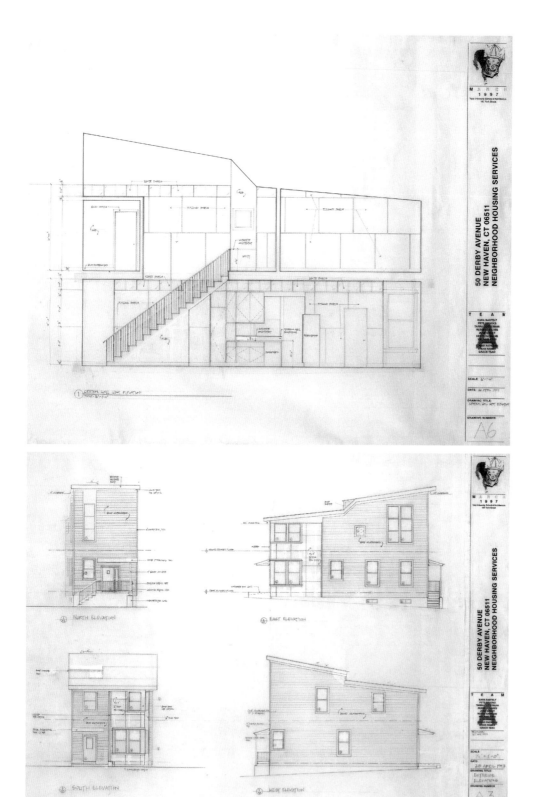

MARCH
1997
Yale University School of Architecture
180 York Street

50 DERBY AVENUE
NEW HAVEN, CT 06511
NEIGHBORHOOD HOUSING SERVICES

TEAM
KARA BARTELT
PETE BROOKS
TARINI PARTHASARATHY
RUSSELL HOLCOMBE
KEVIN STACK
ROMAN NAZARETH
CESAR MATHEW
ADAM RANGE
GRACE TSAO

SCALE
DATE: 28 APRIL 1997
DRAWING TITLE:
CRITICAL WALL SECT. ELEVATION
DRAWING NUMBER:
A6

1 CRITICAL WALL SECT. ELEVATION
SCALE: 1/2" = 1'-0"

MARCH
1997
Yale University School of Architecture
180 York Street

50 DERBY AVENUE
NEW HAVEN, CT 06511
NEIGHBORHOOD HOUSING SERVICES

TEAM
KARA BARTELT
PETE BROOKS
TARINI PARTHASARATHY
RUSSELL HOLCOMBE
KEVIN STACK
ROMAN NAZARETH
CESAR MATHEW
ADAM RANGE
GRACE TSAO

SCALE
DATE: 28 APRIL 1997
DRAWING TITLE:
EXTERIOR ELEVATIONS
DRAWING NUMBER:
A3

NORTH ELEVATION

EAST ELEVATION

SOUTH ELEVATION

WEST ELEVATION

previous spread:
Exterior view.
opposite: Working
drawings showing a section
and elevations.
above: Rear and side
elevations of the
completed building.

The 1998 building project, a house at the corner of Sherman and Gilbert Avenues, was an exercise in balancing contradictory goals: matching the scale of neighboring multi-family homes with a 1,500-square-foot house; commanding a prominent corner lot while offering seclusion; and embracing contemporary architectural ideas in an accessible manner.

The site was in a run-down residential community near the Hospital of Saint Raphael, about a mile west of the architecture school and one block from the 1997 and 1999 projects. The surrounding houses are massive, unkempt Victorians, bulked up with the typical accoutrements — turrets, porticoes and finials — of once-affluent Sherman Avenue. To fit into this existing context, the students inflated the scale of the new residence with higher-than-average ceilings, a steeply pitched roof, a raised first floor, and an L-shaped plan massed at the street corner.

Acknowledging their task's dual demands — community reinvigoration and individual retreat — the designers endeavored to create a residence that would be inviting but secure. To that end, they built a wrap-around porch on the two street-facing façades, expressing openness while providing a layer of protection.

The plan of the house is a shallow L-shape that allows every major room to have views of both the street and the yard, admitting light from at least two directions. The space between the legs of the 'L' holds a private outdoor deck, accessible from the kitchen and living room.

As the students developed and carried out their conceptual program, they discovered a useful metaphor to help express their ideas about privacy and publicity: an unpeeled orange with a pulled-out quarter section. Architecturally, a layer of clapboard cladding symbolizing the "rind" is furred-out three and a half inches from the house's board-and-batten walls — the "flesh" of the orange. The clapboard rind is seen only on the public sides of the house, although it stops short of the roof, calling attention to its rhetorical nature. To complete the metaphor, the private deck area, rendered like a slice removed from the volume of the house, has board-and-batten walls: the flesh is exposed, and by extension, the private is made public.

One design detail had a serendipitous origin. Class member Sonya Hals was a student in a graduate seminar taught by Kent Bloomer called "Actual 3-D." The class made a field trip Mystic Seaport to learn how wooden boats are formed. At Mystic, Hals discovered deck prisms — pyramidal chunks of glass set into ships' decks to bring light below — and conceived the idea to set a prism into the concrete basement wall of the building project house. Working with classmate Tim Hickman, she built a cone-shaped wood case around a prism and placed it in the formwork for one of the walls before the concrete was poured. The result is a bright fan of daylight across the landing of the basement staircase.
— Tim Hickman and TW

project: House at 96 Sherman Avenue

location: New Haven, Connecticut
client: Neighborhood Housing Services of New Haven

previous spread: Street
façade.
above and opposite:
Construction views.

opposite: T. A. Adam
Hopfner and high school
intern.
top left: Detail of the porch
roof underside.
bottom left: Detail of the
basement prism.

The decline in New Haven's population from its high watermark of the 1950s resulted in a 'de-densification' of many neighborhoods, and a number of large, open lots. The vacant lots — formerly the site of multiple family dwellings or multiple freestanding structures, as in the 1999 site — present a challenge to developers seeking to meet a need for smaller single-family homes, while simultaneously aiming to fill holes in the urban fabric.

In addition to the site's large size, the first-year students faced the added challenge of designing for a corner at the intersection of Judson and Winthrop Avenues. These difficulties, however, inspired an eponymous massing strategy. The "Wedge," as the 1999 building project is known, creates the illusion of scale, expanding almost two-fold from its façade to its rear. The gabled roof enhances the illusion as well, growing dramatically outward and upward, in essence, "flaring the structure's tail feathers." In this way, the small building is able to command its large lot.

The designers' wedge form not only speaks to social issues, but creates the opportunity for a less traditional, more open interior. Their massing strategy also addresses the problem of building a contemporary home in a strongly traditional setting. The team's use of vernacular exterior details, such as a gabled roof and front porch similar to others in the area, help reconcile the building with its surroundings.

The 1999 building also challenges the technical and material norms of previous houses, implementing notable strategies to improve upon the quality of the project. The class researched both typical and atypical construction materials and assessed their economic, environmental, and social impacts. Subsequently, specific manufacturers were introduced to the project, with many ultimately donating both time and materials.

The exterior wall construction exemplifies the innovative strategies used throughout: a ventilated rain screen minimizes moisture damage by reducing the air pressure differential across the wall assembly — moisture that does find its way into the wall is given an escape route, thus keeping the wall dry; cementitious clapboards are held three-quarters of an inch from the sheathing; all exterior details around openings, at the foundation, and at the eaves allow for the movement of air into and out of the cavity; and open-cell spray foam insulation minimizes air infiltration and provides improved thermal resistance.

To maintain a healthy interior environment, interior millwork is constructed with formaldehyde-free, medium-density fiberboard, and all interior paints are low-VOC. Custom-fabricated steel assemblies include an interior stair guardrail and interior and exterior structural connection details. Sliding translucent panels separate the kitchen from the dining and living rooms, allowing for greater functional flexibility on the first floor. Modular bookcases provide storage and serve to define zones within this free-plan. On the second floor, which contains more private spaces, the master bedroom includes a home office that is located in the protruding prow of the wedge.
— Adam Ruedig and Jeff Goldstein

location: New Haven, Connecticut
client: Neighborhood Housing Services of New Haven

project: House at 212 Winthrop Avenue

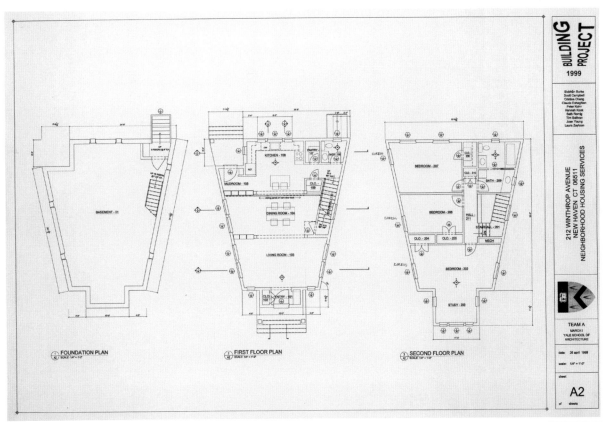

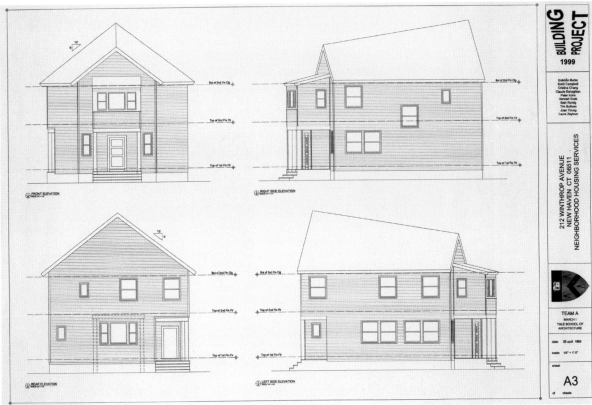

previous spread:
Exterior view.
opposite: Construction view.
above: Working drawings
showing plans and elevations.

In 2000, the first-year students were given a narrow lot with a tall willow tree at the corner of West Read and Watson Streets in New Haven. The winning team focused on two challenges: creating privacy for the homeowner on a site with two street-facing elevations, and preserving the existing trees and shrubs.

The site, located on a block east of Dixwell Avenue just a few hundred yards from the border of Hamden, is a neighborhood with a proud African-American history, although in recent decades its story is one characterized by poverty and violence fueled, in part, by the withering of the nearby Winchester Arms factory. The area is filled with turn-of-the-century working-class homes typical of New Haven, although directly across from the 2000 site is a newer one-story church. The configuration of one-way streets around the site makes it very quiet, with relatively little traffic.

Reflecting the designers' interest in preserving the existing flora, the footprint is configured so that the foundation does not threaten the root system of the big willow tree. Other indigenous plants were carefully removed and stored during construction, and the redesign of the yard accommodated their replanting when construction was completed. The end result is a contemporary house set in an attractively mature landscape.

To increase the layered privacy afforded by the preserved landscape, the designers built a porch along the length of the house and placed stairs at both ends. On the narrow West Read Street façade, the porch cuts into the first floor and extends beyond it before stepping down to grade. It is an accommodating gesture echoed by the upward tilt of the roof above the porch. Although these mark the entrance to the property, one actually has to continue to the center of the long side to reach the front door. Inside, the visitor has arrived at the central point of circulation — a double-height space containing the stair. The plan radiates from this core.

The building section responds to the geometry of the roof and plan. As the roof rises from back to front, the second floor steps up as it passes the stair, bending like the plan. The result is high ceilings and large windows in the master bedroom on the second floor, as well as in the living room below.

The designers used conventional materials in innovative ways, streamlining the house's tectonic elaboration. For example, the clapboard wraps around the corners in a continuous fashion, eliminating the need for corner boards. To ensure that this condition is visible from the street, the porch has no railings, since the floor level of the porch is just under the height at which a rail would be required. Painted in creamy marigold tones, the house is a distinctive presence on its block.

Several new construction products and technologies were introduced to the Building Project in 2000, a trend that began in earnest in 1999 and continues in more recent houses. For the first time, a standing-seam metal roof was specified and could be installed by the students, unlike the asphalt-shingle roofs of previous houses. The class also became interested in shop fabrication, and manufactured a black walnut and aluminum staircase in the School of Architecture woodshop. Access to its controlled environment and precision tools allowed the students to become more ambitious with their material selection and detailing because elements such as the staircase could be built concurrently with the house. This allowed work to proceed on two or more tracks simultaneously.
— TW

location: New Haven, Connecticut
client: Neighborhood Housing Services of New Haven

project: House at 23 West Read Street

2000

previous spread:
Street façade.
above: Construction view
with Brian Papa, Ameet
Hiremath, and Derek Warr.
opposite: Working
drawings showing plans
and elevations.

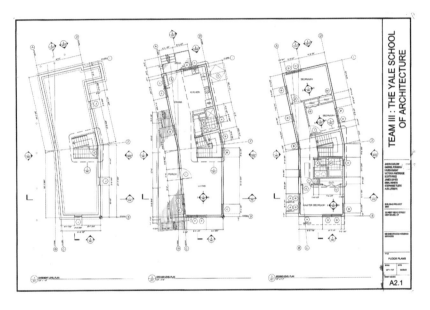

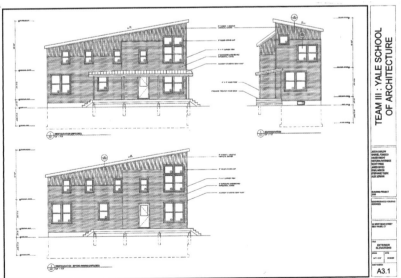

above: Opening celebration.
opposite: Side elevation.

The 2001 building project, which sits on a double site at the corner of Fifth Street and Hallock Avenue, is highly visible from the I-95 freeway. While it was important that the house fit in with the local vernacular, it was also presumed that the house could develop its own building forms. The design takes into consideration diverse needs: for privacy, formal integration into the neighborhood, and use of the site's full potential.

The initial design team, composed of four women and one man, wanted the 1,500-square-foot house to relate to the larger landscape of Long Island Sound, as well as the more intimate precincts of the property and neighborhood. More public and semi-public areas, such as the living room and kitchen, are oriented toward the former, while private spaces such as the bedrooms face the more intimate back yard. A small living room and balcony are located upstairs and face Long Island Sound to the north, allowing a programmatic element to be enjoyed by all members of the household and creating an acoustic and visual buffer for two upstairs bedrooms. The upper volume aligns with the adjacent house, maintaining a consistent street edge.

The downstairs volume is shifted thirty degrees and offset from the upstairs spaces, making the house feel larger than it is, and enabling all surfaces to organize the covering for the structure's wrap-around deck. This relates visually to neighboring houses with similar porches. In the rear, the house turns away from the street toward the back in the form of a "C," creating an intimate zone. At the front is a secondary living room for entertaining adjacent to a kitchen/eating area arranged in an open plan. The main bedroom is located downstairs in a less traditional, secluded placement, allowing it to serve double-duty as guest bedroom or home office.

The 2001 project was the first house in New Haven to use what is known as a non-vented "hot roof." The Icynene spray foam insulation used in the roof and walls is not permeable by air and does not require venting, resulting in a thermally tighter, more energy-efficient structure that achieves a Five-Star Energy rating. Another technical innovation specified by the students was prefabricated concrete basement walls with integrated insulation, built off-site and positioned with a crane.

This 2001 building project house was purchased by a neighborhood family during the framing phase of construction, indicating an acceptance and desire on the part of the community for less traditional building forms, which was very gratifying for the students.
— April Marie Clark

location: New Haven, Connecticut
client: Neighborhood Housing Services of New Haven

project: House at 33 Fifth Street

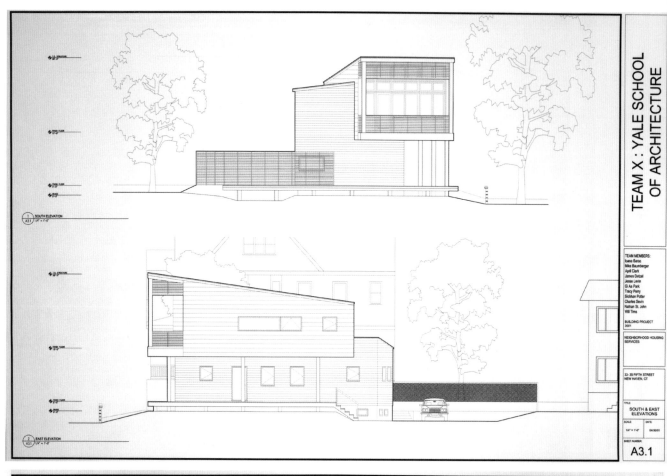

SOUTH ELEVATION
A3.1 1/4" = 1'-0"

EAST ELEVATION
A3.1 1/4" = 1'-0"

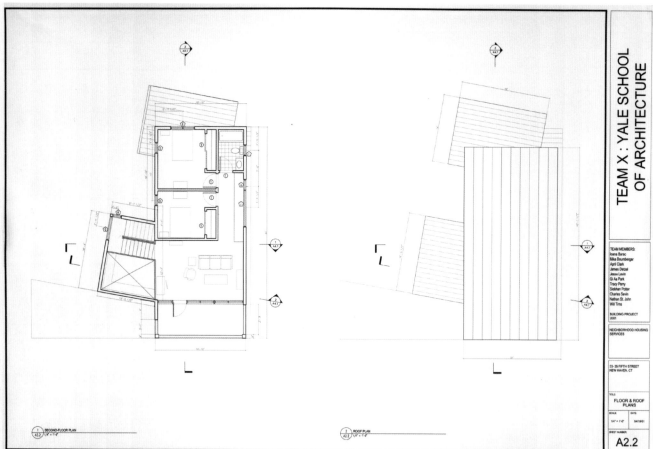

SECOND-FLOOR PLAN
A2.2 1/4" = 1'-0"

ROOF PLAN
A2.2 1/4" = 1'-0"

previous spread: Exterior
view from street.
opposite: Working drawings
showing elevations and
second floor and roof plans.
right: Exterior detail.

The 2002 project is a single-family house on a double-width lot at the corner of two residential streets in New Haven, Parmelee Avenue and Porter Street. Parallel to the property in the rear, one of the city's main traffic arteries, Route 34 (the Oak Street Connector), can be seen in the distance. An empty lot to the west separates the house from its neighbors.

The students developed an environmentally sensitive concept for this project, incorporating strategies to use solar orientation, natural ventilation, and passive cooling in its design. They placed the mass of the 1,500-square-foot house on the east side of the lot in order to maximize open space. The house has a narrow south façade on Porter Street and a long east elevation on Parmelee Avenue. In contrast to most houses in the neighborhood which have gable roofs, the 2002 project has a shed roof.

A service core of bathrooms, kitchen, stairs, and storage areas consolidated along the east side of the house creates an elongated, continuous zone on the west side of the house, culminating in a double-height living room. Turning its back on the distant Oak Street Connector, the interior volume opens to the large side yard on the west through sliding glass doors leading to a raised deck.

The focal point of the living space is a switchback stair articulated by a custom-designed, partial-height shelving unit. Prefabricated in birch plywood in the School of Architecture woodworking shop and outfitted with integral lighting, the cabinet serves as a bookcase and display unit. Backed by translucent corrugated plastic panels, it also acts like an illuminated screen, creating shadow play when people climb up and down the steps.

Overlooking the double-height volume, a large hallway on the second floor is used as a study or play area. Partitions with interior clerestory windows separate this space from the three bedrooms. While maintaining privacy, these interior clerestories admit natural light into the bedrooms, which are open to the underside of the shed roof. The two smaller bedrooms have paired closets conceived as a single piece of cabinetry.

The house is wood-frame construction sheathed in clapboards. The roof is composed of composite wood beams and insulated panels covered in standing-seam, galvanized aluminum roofing. East-facing clerestory windows admit indirect light, while the deep overhang of the roof mitigates direct sunlight.

A freestanding wall of horizontal cedar planking divides the driveway from the raised deck. A combination storage/seating element with a built-in bench enhances its utility. The house, painted a deep barn red, has become a landmark on the Route 34 corridor near the Ella Grasso Boulevard.
— MB

location: New Haven, Connecticut
client: Neighborhood Housing Services of New Haven

project: House at 83 Parmelee Avenue

previous spread:
Exterior view.
above, left and opposite:
Construction views.

opposite and above:
Interior views.

above: Side elevation.
right top: Opening
celebration.
right bottom: Dean Robert
A.M. Stern, James Paley,
Henry Dynia, and Paul
Brouard with Adam Hopfner
and community residents.

In 2003, students faced the challenge of designing a residence next door to the house built the year before. In 2002, the site was a double-width corner lot at the corner of Porter Street and Parmelee Avenue. In 2003, in contrast, the inside lot was a narrow one. This location, combined with the presence of past Building Project houses in the surrounding blocks of the West River neighborhood, highlighted the theme of contextualization for the students.

The class designed a 1,500-square-foot, two-story house that expresses distinctions between the interior and exterior, public and private areas, work and leisure zones, and man-made and natural boundaries. The house is organized around a central service and circulation core composed of the kitchen, bathroom, storage areas, and staircase. Paneled in plywood articulated by a grid of reveals, the core bisects the building, with main spaces located on either side: the living room in the front and the dining area in the back. From the dining area, sliding-glass doors open onto a rear deck intended to merge with the back yard.

On the second floor, the master bedroom and two smaller bedrooms are organized around the core elements of bathroom, closets, storage, and an open loft space with a built-in window seat. The exterior side of the core is articulated by a glazed wall of custom windows fitted with adjustable wooden louvers.

Cementitious clapboards donated by the manufacturer, James Hardie Siding, sheath all but the service and circulation core, which is clad in stained plywood paneling. Other distinctive elements on the elevations include the cantilevered core at the south façade, where it appears suspended above a garden in the side yard. On the north, the plywood paneling identifies a side entrance with an overhead canopy. The custom-designed louvered windows also highlight the staircase from the exterior. Large, double-hung stock windows contrast with the custom glazing.

Landscaping features include a paved driveway, a pathway composed of six-inch-square pavers that connects the front entrance to the sidewalk, low shrubbery at the border of the lawn, and a wood fence that serves double-duty as built-in storage for trash and garden equipment. As a special amenity, the class designed and planted a fenced-in herb garden just outside the kitchen door. Located in a neighborhood where most fences are chain-link, and where little is done to soften the transition from the street to the houses, these modest additions contribute to the care expressed in the overall design of the project.
— Vanessa Ruff

location: New Haven, Connecticut
client: Neighborhood Housing Services of New Haven

project: House at 161 Porter Street

previous spread: Exterior
view.
top left: Jennifer Newsom at
the final design review.
bottom left: Design models.
above: Robert A.M. Stern,
Brian Healy, Alan Organschi,
Mark Simon, and Joseph
Weisbord of Housing First
New York with students.

2003 / 239

above top: Vanessa Ruff and
Noah Shepard.
above bottom and opposite:
Construction views.

opposite: Interior views.
right: Exterior details.

When first-year members of the class of 2006 visited the proposed site of their building project, they initially experienced a shock. While almost all of the houses in the program had been in lower-income neighborhoods, no other project had had a jail as its neighbor. The house is located on Hudson Street between an abandoned one-story building and a public garden, close to the busy route of Whalley Avenue and across the street from the New Haven Correctional Center. The students' challenge was to design a house that offered its occupants maximum privacy and minimum exposure to the jail, while contributing to the neighborhood streetscape.

The design selected was a long and narrow rectangular house, one-story tall at its front and two stories at its rear. To maximize privacy, a ten-foot-high wood screen separates a two-car driveway from a protected deck and side yard at the north side of the house. Combined with the concrete wall of the abandoned building next door, the screen creates a private, exterior courtyard.

In contrast to previous houses in the program, the Hudson Street house occupies primarily one floor. Two bedrooms are located at the rear of the first floor, while one bedroom and a bathroom are placed on a partial second floor. The living space expands in height from the single-story kitchen at one end to an eighteen-foot-tall volume at the other. The designers intended the kitchen and living room to be perceived as one space, separated only by an eight-foot-long dining bar. Windows along the south wall look onto the adjacent public garden, while glass sliding doors along the north wall open onto the protected deck and side yard.

This house is the first project in the history of the program to take advantage of computer numerically controlled (CNC) technology. Students used this technology in the design of the staircase that extends from the basement to the second floor. A cabinet-like structure, it is best appreciated from the double-height volume of the living room. After developing a series of test joints and prototypes using the CNC laser cutter, the students designed a matrix based on the dimensions of the staircase treads and risers. An egg-crate joint allows the treads and risers to serve as shelves and storage for the homeowner's television, stereo, books, and laundry. Five students worked on the design of the staircase, which they analyzed into component pieces that could fit on four-by-eight-foot plywood sheets. A total of thirty-nine sheets of plywood were cut, sanded, and finished at Breakfast Woodworks, a custom millwork shop in Guilford owned by Yale alumnus Louis Mackall, who was a pioneer of design-build practice in the 1960s.

This year's class, the largest class in the program's history, was responsible for every part of the construction, which began in May and continued through the end of August. Twelve students worked through the summer to finish the siding, painting, and interior finishes.

Two types of window trim activate the façade. Three-inch-deep cedar boxes frame large openings along the north and south façades, while wide, flat boards painted dark blue — the same color as the siding — surround smaller windows. Whereas the deep trim accentuates the large apertures, the flat trim causes the smaller windows to blend with the building's surface. A two-foot-deep cedar window bay in the kitchen acts like a lens, simultaneously distancing the house's occupants from the jail, while framing views of trees across the street. Along with generously sized front and side porches, the window bay contributes to the neighborly aspect of the house on the street.
— Abigail Ransmeier

location: New Haven, Connecticut
client: Neighborhood Housing Services of New Haven

project: House at 18 Hudson Street

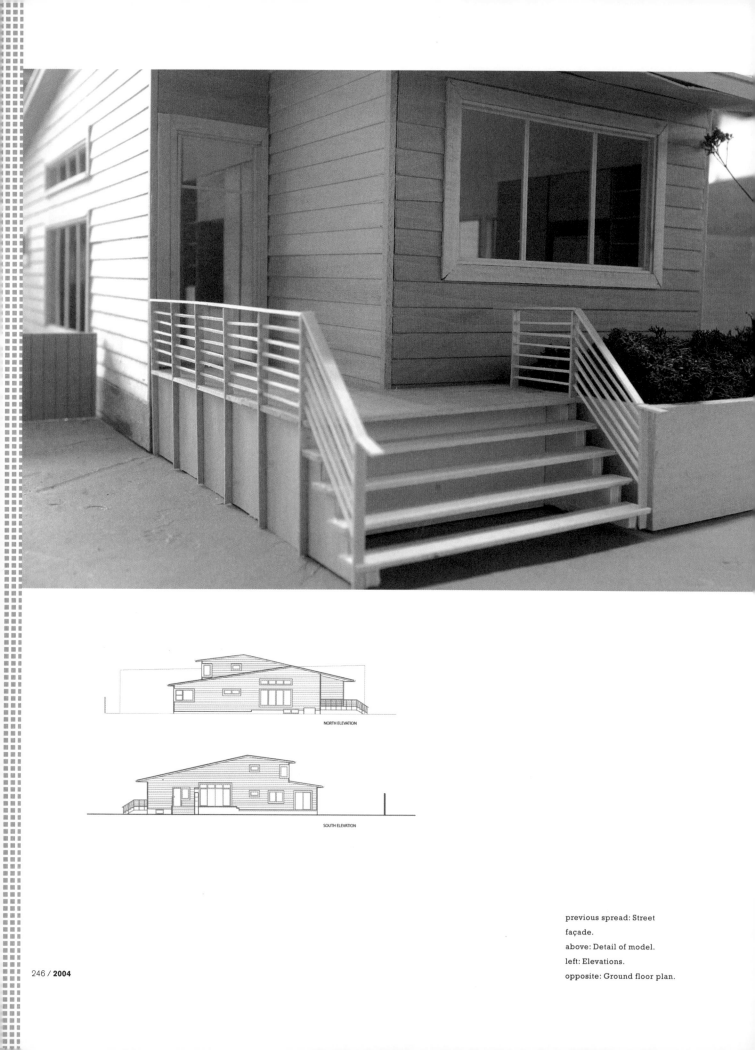

NORTH ELEVATION

SOUTH ELEVATION

previous spread: Street
façade.
above: Detail of model.
left: Elevations.
opposite: Ground floor plan.

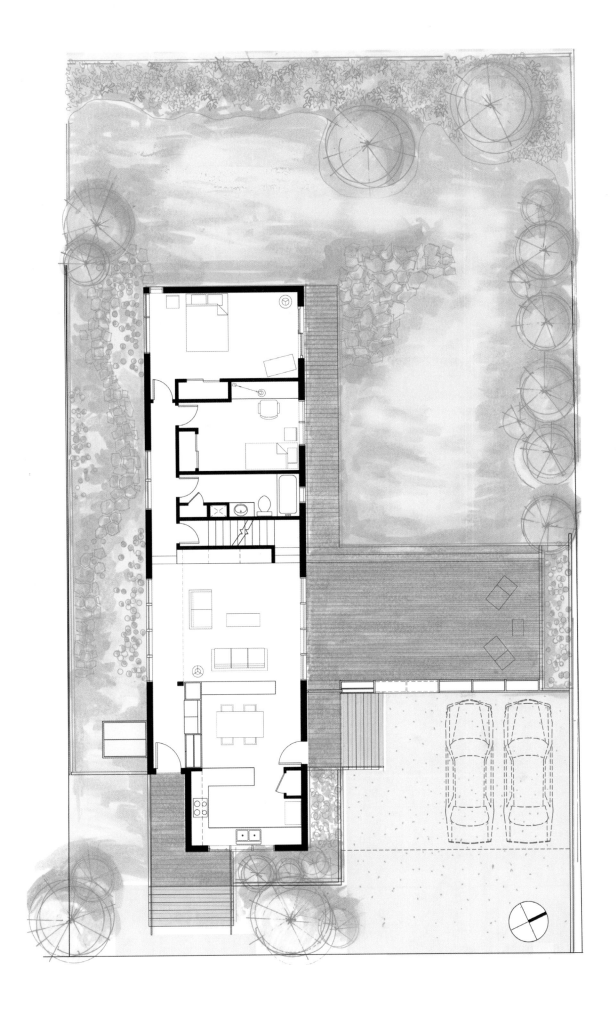

above and opposite:
Construction views.

above: Detail of prefabricated storage unit with
faculty members Alan
Organschi and Amy
Lelyveld.
opposite: Exterior views.

At first glance, the 2005 building project may seem simple and restrained, especially in comparison to its predecessors. The symmetrical façade with four large windows and a gable roof appears calm, and the dark tea color blends quietly into the Orchard Street surroundings. On closer inspection, however, one begins to understand the programmatic orientation and geometric complexity, as a truer picture of the design emerges.

This refined sensibility may be the result of the project's unique beginning and the interest by the class of 2007 in sustainability and renewable energy. An educational grant from the Connecticut Clean Energy Fund permitted the inclusion of photovoltaic panels, marking another first in the history of the Yale Building Project. Solar panels located on the roof provide energy both for the house and for the City of New Haven, extending the impact of the grant from the homeowner to the larger community.

Lined with many large multi-family dwellings, Orchard Street presented a challenging location for the 1,500-square-foot house. Students built up the mass of the front of the house by orienting private spaces to the street: the master bedroom on the ground floor and two smaller bedrooms upstairs. Placed at the back of the house, the living and dining rooms are combined into one large volume open to the sloping roof above, making the interior feel larger than it really is, and extending into a partially covered exterior deck. A dynamic roof, which transforms from a high frontal gable to a low shed roof at the back, provides a plane for the photovoltaic panel system that is calibrated for maximum solar exposure. Class member Brook Denison notes that Kent Bloomer's class on geometry helped students in their design of the twisting roof. A standing-seam aluminum roofing system made of malleable, twenty-four-inch-wide panels accentuates the dynamic form.

Although the house changes shape dramatically from the street to the back yard, a consistent material, Hardie plank siding, creates a unified skin. This envelope is interrupted at key moments by openings lined with recycled materials serving double functions. Cowl-like projections shade the south-facing windows and create a canopy at the main entrance, located near the middle of the south-facing side elevation. This entrance leads directly to the heart of the house, which contains the service core of kitchen, storage, and full bathroom.

On the interior, narrow strips of whitewashed birch plywood, nailed onto sheets of black plastic and separated by quarter-inch spacing, create geometric lines that highlight the ceiling's complex shape. A large skylight on the north side of the ceiling plane floods the living room with even daylight, and offers a view of a magnificent tree. A shear wall located at the center of the house, designed in conjunction with Ed Stanley, a structural engineer and lecturer in the School of Architecture, extends from the basement to the roof, providing lateral stability.

While social and environmental concerns were the driving force behind the design, constructing the house was focused on teamwork. Systematic techniques were developed for repetitive tasks, leading to efficient installations and an accelerated learning curve. Lengthy discussions with manufacturers led to collaborative solutions to many complex, custom details. In the end, the 2005 building project was an educational endeavor focused on a diverse range of issues, including feasibility and constructability. Thus, some of the most important aspects of the design are contained within its process, as if residing beneath the surface of the house.
— Marc Guberman

2005

location: New Haven, Connecticut
client: Neighborhood Housing Services of New Haven

project: House at 590 Orchard Street

previous spread: Exterior
view.
top left: Student Harris Ford
presents project.
bottom left: Models.
above: Final design review.
From left: Mark Simon, Alec
Purves, Keith Krumwiede,
and Robert A.M. Stern with
James Paley and Brian Healy
in background.

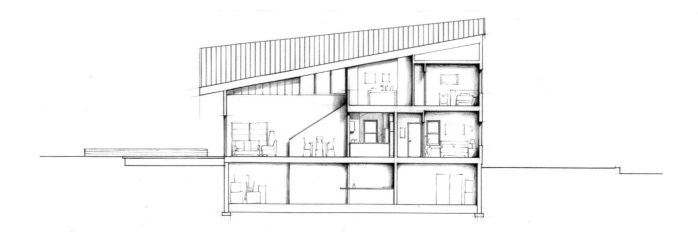

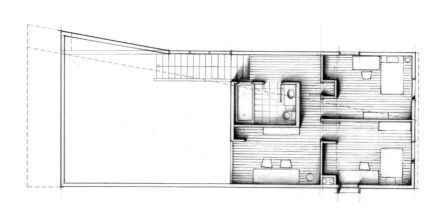

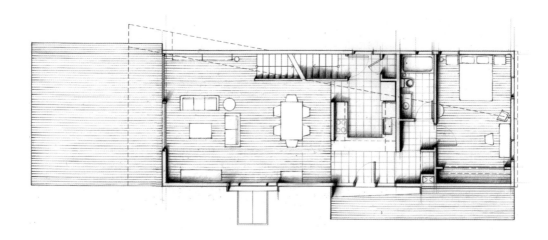

above: Section and
floor plans.
opposite: Christopher Lee
(top) and Seung Namgoong
(bottom).

opposite and above: Interior
and exterior views of
the completed building.
below: Elevation.

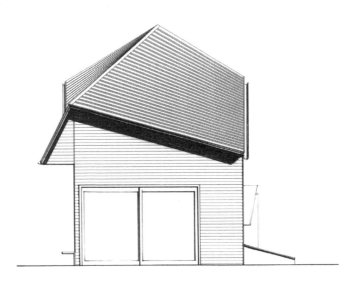

Detail is what you notice as you walk through the 2006 building project — expressing an idea, unifying two rooms, or resolving a material intersection. But, for all of the meticulous effort by many authors that the details express, the 2006 design retains its original, driving concepts, the most important of which was to strike a balance between interior and exterior spaces.

The 2006 project occupies a distinctive lot among multi-family houses and apartment buildings on Henry Street in New Haven's Dixwell neighborhood. Nearly double-wide, with a five-foot drop in grade and a sixty-foot-tall Norway Maple tree at its heart, the site offered challenges and opportunities that guided the students in their design. Landscaping and exterior construction extend the design beyond the 1,500-square-foot program across the property. On the ground floor, each interior room was designed to connect with an exterior counterpart, and balance indoor and outdoor volumes, suggesting possibilities for different areas of the yard. The massing of the house encloses a large outdoor room by framing the canopy of the tree, giving the outdoor shaded area both prominence and shelter. A solid wall to the west near the property line is designed as a shell that shelters the interior volumes from the neighboring house.

A double-height interior void creates a vertical core from which all other living areas spin off, and the interior arrangement reflects the site. As these spaces open to the east and north, revealing both the maple tree and the suggested exterior "rooms," the floor level steps down with each change in function, accentuating the existing grade and mediating between the street front and back yard. Details articulate these design ideas and the use of materials is intended to unify disparate elements. Horizontal slatted cedar fencing around an outdoor patio is reincarnated as siding for solid benches on the back deck. Aluminum channels used at the joints of the exterior cladding are also used in fence posts and toe-kicks at an exterior bench. Ship-lapped cedar siding highlights the exposed shell of the west perimeter walls and roof soffits, and reappears at the front porch, which is carved into the mass of the building. A custom-designed steel and cedar handrail at the interior staircase connects the spaces on the second floor to lower levels and to the exterior porches through the use of like materials and handling.

The details of this project also represent figurative ideas and accentuate fine-grained design elements. An ornamental screen at the perimeter of the double-height space, for example, is assembled from milled cedar boards with a solid-and-void pattern based on the maple tree. The screen underlines the importance of the tree and its interior counterpart — the vertical volume — and adds a contemporary take on ornament within a context resplendent with traditional architectural flourishes. Beech countertops form a continuous datum throughout the first floor, physically connecting each room, while forming a visual separation from the kitchen. Routed wood vents, cabinets with reveals, and slotted siding all particularize different spaces and elements in the house.

Some details are pragmatic. Built-in cabinetry, which students fabricated in the wood workshop at the School of Architecture, provides storage throughout the house. The double-height slot offers an auditory connection between the two floors, as well as between the utility entrance and the rest of the house. Continuing the efforts of previous classes to be environmentally responsible, the 2006 house incorporates solar panels on the roof, natural ventilation through operable windows in each room, reclaimed bluestone curbs as landscaping material, and a large variety of native trees and plants replacing invasive species throughout the property.

Whether it is the larger vision of the design, or the precision of its finely wrought details, there is an enthusiasm evident in the 2006 house that we hope will endure as the Yale Building Project moves forward.
— Benjamin Smoot

location: New Haven, Connecticut
client: Neighborhood Housing Services of New Haven

project: House at 51 Henry Street

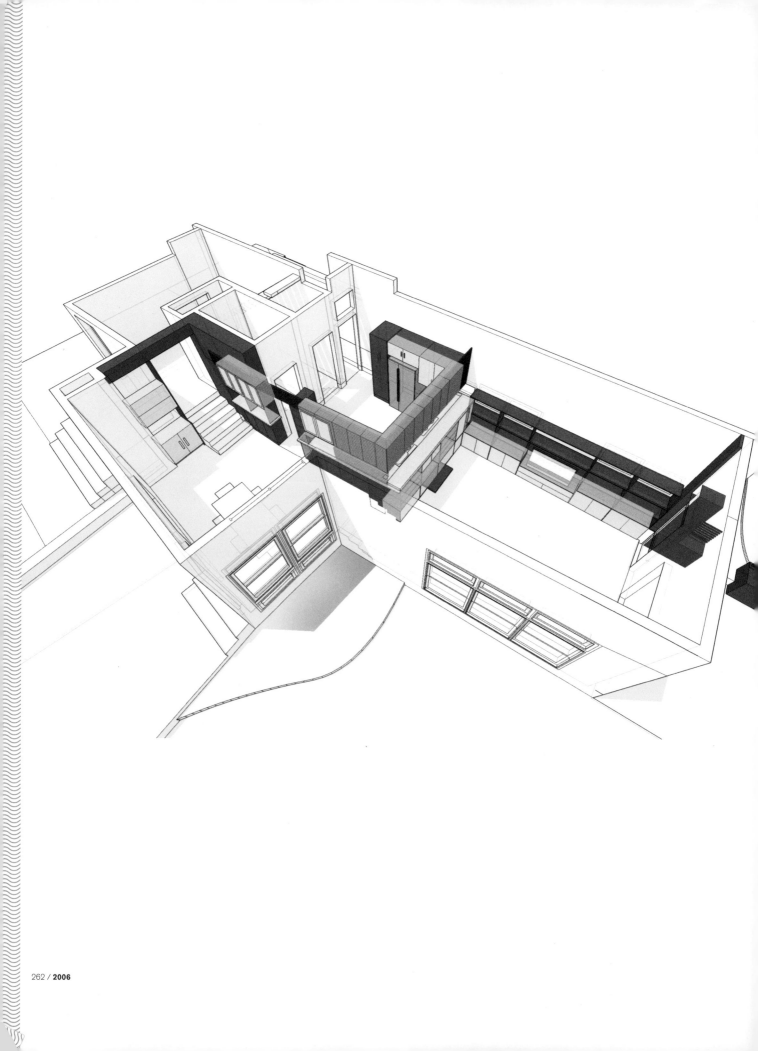

previous spread:
Exterior view.
opposite: Rendering of
interior perspective.
above: Exterior rendering.

opposite and above:
Construction views.

opposite: Jessica Lupo,
Michael Krop, and Paul
Brouard.
above: Exterior view of the
completed building.

above: Rear and side
façades.
right: Opening celebration.
opposite: Detail of the
completed house.

Alumni Acknowledgments

The following graduates of the Yale School of
Architecture, listed according to their class year,
assisted in the preparation of this book:

1951   Peter Millard

1961   Paul B. Brouard

1962   Tai Soo Kim

1964   M.J. Long

1965   Thomas Hall Beeby, Peter L. Gluck, David
       E. Sellers, and Robert A.M. Stern

1967   Glenn H. Gregg and Herbert S. Newman

1968   Lawrence H. Goltz

1969   William H. Grover, William B. Richardson,
       Robert Swenson, and Paul J. Thompson

1970   Turner Brooks, F. Andrus Burr, Roc
       Caivano, Tom Carey, Michael Curtis,
       Richard K. Dozier, Steve Edwins,
       Ronald C. Filson, John Jacobson, James V.
       Righter, Robert W. Knight, and
       Peter Kurt Woerner

1971   Stephen J.L. Douglas, Terry Gips,
       Steven Heikin, Ellen Leopold, Robert L.
       Miller, Robert D. Nicolais, and
       Susan St. John

1972   Gerald Allen, Mark Appleton, Richard
       Nash Gould, Mark L. Hildebrand,
       Marvin Michalsen, Jefferson B. Riley,
       Richard C. Shepard, Jr., Mark Simon,
       and Brinkley Thorne

1973   Judy Bing, Thomas L. Doremus, Chad
       Floyd, Robert P. Hammell, Everardo A.
       Jefferson, Nancy Monroe, Donald Raney,
       R. Jerome Wagner, Christopher Woerner,
       and Buzz Yudell

1974   William P. Durkee IV, Robert Godley,
       Eleftherios Pavlides, Patrick L. Pinnell,
       David M. Schwarz, David S. Soleau, and
       Michael G. Timchula

1975   Karyn M. Gilvarg, Susan Godshall,
       Andrew K. Stevenson, and J. David
       Waggonner III

1976   C. Douglas Ballon, Robert S. Charney,
       Barbara R. Feibelman, James Kessler,
       William A. McDonough, Eric Jay Oliner,
       Carolyn W. Silk, and Barry Svigals

1977   Calvert Bowie, Eric Epstein, Barbara
       Flanagan, Jonathan S. Kammel,
       Kevin Lichten, Laura Jane Lintz, and
       Andrew Robinson

1978   John B. Connell, William S. Mead, and
       William Hall Paxson

1979   Patrick C. Hickox, Richard McElhiney,
       Robert Olson, and Melanie Taylor

1980   Stephen W. Harby, Robert S. Kahn, Mariko
       Masuoka, Ann K. McCallum,
       Kari R. Nordstrom, Reese T. Owens, and
       Michael Zenreich

1981   Michael Cadwell, Mitchell A. Hirsch,
       Jane Murphy, and Martin Shofner

1982   Thomas A. Kligerman, Kay Bea Jones,
       John Kaliski, Nate McBride, William H.
       Sherman, and Wendy Westfall Franzen

1983   Aaron A. Betsky, Carol J. Burns, Stuart
       Christenson, William H. Gilliss, and
       Robert N. Works

1984   Bruce R. Becker, Jill S. Riley, Paul M.
       Rosenblatt, and David Scheer

1985   Barbara A. Ball, Glynis M. Berry, Charles
       H. Loomis, and Christine Theodoropoulos

1986   Carey Feierabend, Bruce M. Lindsey,
       Madeline K. Schwartzman, and
       Diane Westerback

1987   Lisa Gray, David B. Hotson, and
       Jennifer Tate

1988   Andrew Berman, Bruce Graham, and
       Alan W. Organschi

1989   Darin C. Cook

1990   Matt Bucy, Roberto J. Espejo, and
       Andrea Warchaizer

1991   Alisa Dworsky, John Gilmer, Diana
       Greenberg, Alec Stuart, Claire Theobald,
       and Michael Wetstone

1992   Daniel Sagan and Mark Sofield

1993   Christopher Arelt, Gregory Barnell,
       Louise Harpman and Gitta Robinson

1994   John L. Culman and Michael Knopoff

1995   George Knight

1996   Michael Koch and Mai-Tse Wu

1997   Alexander Barrett and Jennifer
       Smith Lewis

1999   Tarra Cotterman and Adam Hopfner

2000   Tim Hickman Sonya Hals, and Ted Whitten

2001   Jeff Goldstein and Adam Ruedig

2002   Dee Briggs, Joseph Ferrucci, and
       Victoria Partridge

2003   April Marie Clark

2005   Marissa Brown, Ruth Gyuse,
       and Vanessa Ruff

2006   Andrew Lyon and Abigail Ransmeier

2007   Benjamin Smoot

2008   Tim Applebee and Marc Guberman

Image Credits

Avery Architectural Fine Arts Library, p. 14 (middle, bottom) 15 (top) and 18 (top, bottom), *Progressive Architecture*, May 1966, p. 20 (bottom), 38 (bottom)

Bruce R. Becker, p. 118

Kent Bloomer, p. 64, 67, 69

Michael Caldwell, p. 37 (top), 61

Aubrey Carter, p. 138, 140 (bottom), 141, 142, 143

Centerbrook Architects and Planners, p. 13

Charles W. Moore Center for the Study of Place, p. 11, 16 (bottom), 17, 20 (top, middle), 46 (top)

Michael Curtis, p. 27 (bottom)

Elizabeth Ives School, p. 81

Mark Ellis, p. 21 (bottom)

Wendy Westfall Franzen, p. 32 (top), 106 (top)

Peter L. Gluck, p. 14 (top)

Susan Godshall, p. 66 (middle, bottom), 72

Habitat for Humanity of Greater New Haven, p. 39

Richard W. Hayes, p. 157

Ellen Leopold, p. 21(top), 26 (top, second)

Interiors, December 1968, p 22 (middle, bottom), 23, 50, 52, 53, 54

Jim Kessler, p. 78, 80

Kevin Lichten, p. 31 (bottom), 37 (bottom)]

Manuscripts and Archives, Yale University, p. 26 (third, fourth), 37 (middle), 46 (bottom), 48

Neighborhood Housing Services, p. 238 (bottom), 240 (bottom), 241, 242 (top), 243 (bottom), 244, 248, 249, 251 (bottom), 254 (bottom), 259 (top)

Donald Raney, p. 66 (top)

Gitta Robinson, p. 167 (top)

Madeline Schwartzman, p. 132

Robert Swenson, p. 16 (middle), 22 (top), 55

Brinkley Thorne, p. 58, 59

Michael Timchula, p. 62

West Haven Community House, p. 102

Yale School of Architecture, p. 16 (top), 31 (top, middle), 32 (bottom), 33, 34, 38 (top), 40, 47, 49, 56, 60, 68, 70, 82, 84, 85, 86, 90, 91, 94, 95 (top), 96, 98, 99, 100, 103, 104, 106 (bottom), 107, 108, 109, 110, 112, 113, 114, 115, 116, 119, 120, 121, 122, 124, 125, 126, 127, 128, 130, 131, 133, 134, 136, 137, 144, 146, 147, 148, 149, 150, 152, 153, 154, 156, 158, 161, 167 (bottom), 168, 170, 172, 173, 174, 175, 176, 177, 178, 180, 181(top, right), 182, 183, 184, 185, 186, 188, 189, 190, 191, 192, 194, 195, 196, 198, 200, 201, 202, 203, 204, 206, 207, 208, 211 (bottom), 212, 213 (top), 214, 216, 217, 218, 220, 221, 222, 223, 224, 226, 227, 238 (top), 239, 243 (top), 246 (bottom), 247, 254(top), 255, 256, 259 (bottom), 262, 263

Yale School of Drama, p. 27 (top)

Yale University, Sterling Memorial Library, p. 15 (bottom) *House Beautiful*, July 1966 18 (middle), 19, and 20, *Progressive Architecture*, September 1967, p. 24, *Progressive Architecture*, October 1968, p. 44

Photographs by:

Adrienne Swiatocha, p. 257

Anderson Photography, p. 235

Michael Marsland, p. 160, 181 (left), 228, 230, 231, 232, 233, 234, 236, 240 (top), 242 (bottom), 246 (top), 250, 251 (top)

Ted Whitten, p. 76, 77, 88, 92, 95 (bottom)

Tom Bosschaert, p. 260, 264, 265, 266, 267, 268, 269

Sonya Hals, p. 210, 211 (top), 213 (bottom)

Youngna Park, p. 252, 258

Thank you to all of those who lent us images. While not all could be used in the book, many have been placed in digital, or original form, in the archive of the Building Project housed at Manuscripts and Archives, Yale University Library. If you know of any mistakes in image credits, or have additional information and material for the archive, please contact the Yale School of Architecture.